The Chatsworth Vi

Beeley, Edensor & Pilsley

By Diane Naylor

Foreword by Lord Burlington

To Leslie

love and best wishes

from Diane Naylor xxx

After leaving university, Derbyshire born Diane worked in a design studio in Nottingham. Then in 1984, she began her varied career at Chatsworth and is now responsible for the Photo Library.

Diane is married to David and lives on the Chatsworth estate. She is an avid gardener with an allotment. Her other interests include yoga, walking and scuba diving. Both she and David are keen motorcyclists.

for Naylo

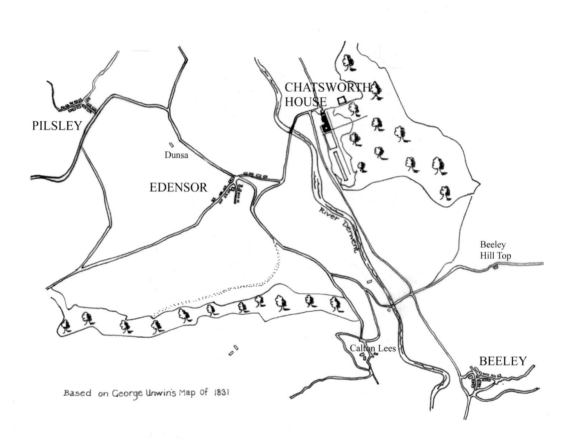

PILSLEY

Dunsa

EDENSOR

CHATSWORTH
HOUSE

River Derwent

Beeley
Hill Top

Calton Lees

BEELEY

Based on George Unwin's Map of 1831

LANDMARK COLLECTOR'S LIBRARY

The Chatsworth Villages
Beeley, Edensor & Pilsley

By Diane Naylor

Foreword by Lord Burlington

Landmark Publishing

Published by

Ashbourne Hall, Cokayne Ave
Ashbourne, Derbyshire DE6 1EJ England
Tel: (01335) 347349 Fax: (01335) 347303
e-mail: landmark@clara.net
web site: www.landmarkpublishing.co.uk

1st edition

ISBN 1-84306-198-8

Printed by Cromwell Press Ltd

Design & reproduction by James Allsopp

Cover captions:

Front cover top: Beeley c.1950
Front cover bottom left: Edensor
Front cover bottom right: Pilsley Well Dressing, 1992
Back cover top: The wedding of Rachel Cavendish, 1923
Back cover bottom left: Beeley football team, 1905
Back cover bottom right: Pilsley School children, 1953
Page 3 top: Edensor Gate House c.1900
Page 3 middle: Coach and horses from Red House Stables, Darley Dale in Pilsley, 1997
Page 3 bottom: Beeley football team, c.1910

CONTENTS

ACKNOWLEDGEMENTS

A special "thank you" must go to Kath Bosett whose enthusiasm for this project persuaded me to undertake it. Sadly Kath died before this book was published. I am particularly indebted to Derek Neave for loaning me his collection of old photographs and to Susan Watts for the use of her father, Hugo Read's archive. All other images have been kindly loaned by estate people with the exception of those credited in the text. Ray Bradshaw's recordings of the oral histories of Dorothy Howard and Ken Simpson were extremely helpful for the Pilsley chapter.

This project has turned in to one involving many people in the community; those that I have bothered during the course of gathering information and photographs include:

The Dowager Duchess of Devonshire
Mark Adams, Stuart & Sue Band, Roy Bosett, Len Broome, Ian Else, Evelyn Aris-Fowkes, Gordon Bowering, Chris Boyce, Liz Bradshaw, Mary Daybell, Rob Dowding, Bridget Flemming, Brian Gilbert, John Grosvenor, Ann Hall, Barbara Hawksworth, Dave & Julia Houghton, Ethel Jackson, Nigel Johnson, Ralph Lord, Charles Noble, Eric & Mary Oliver, Joe & Jill Oliver, John & Margaret Oliver, Derrick & Zoë Penrose, Andrew Peppitt, Sean Read, Frank Robinson, Charlie Roose, Henry Sheldon, David Spencer, Iola Symonds, Stephanie Thraves and Jo Wood.

All must be thanked for their willingness to share information and memories. Thanks must also go to Peter Day and Ian Else for casting their eyes over the text. I had two walking tours both of which were incredibly informative; one of Pilsley with Ralph Lord, Gordon Bowering and Brian Gilbert, and another of Beeley with Frank Robinson on a thundery evening which was enlightening!

Lastly, but most importantly, I must acknowledge, and be grateful for, the unfailing, untiring and good-humoured support of my husband, David, throughout my work on this project.

Diane Naylor, Edensor, 2005.

INTRODUCTION

All three villages are affiliated to Chatsworth; both Edensor and Pilsley are wholly estate villages, and Beeley remains a mixture of privately owned and estate property. This was not always the case as will become apparent in the following pages. Two of the villages have public houses called the Devonshire Arms, two have churches, one has a school and all three once again have shops.

Another thing that all three villages have in common is that no main route runs through them. A conscious decision has to be made to enter the villages to find all that lies within.

FOREWORD

BY LORD BURLINGTON

Although this book was originally conceived as a purely pictorial history, Diane has drawn on her knowledge of the estate gained from working in various departments at Chatsworth for 21 years to create much more than that. With the help of fellow estate employees and others associated with Chatsworth she has put together a book that provides an engrossing narrative, full of little-known facts about the Chatsworth villages that will fascinate natives and visitors alike.

The Lodges on the outskirts of Edensor.

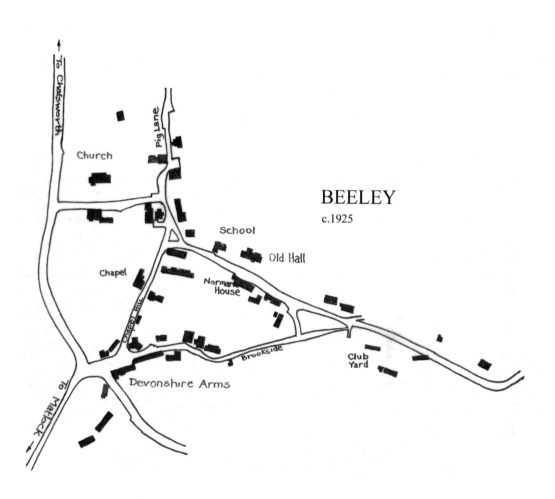

BEELEY

c.1925

BEELEY

The word Beeley is Saxon in origin and it is derived from the name Baega, who may have been the first Saxon chief to settle there, but the word Baega also means a clearing by a bend in a river. On Beeley Moor there is evidence of an early Bronze Age settlement, a tumulus called "Hob Hurst's House" where cremated Saxon human remains have been found. Half a mile from this is a circle of twelve stones 12 yards in diameter. On the edge of the moor is a stone with a square carved out where a wooden cross would once have been fixed. It is thought that this was probably erected to mark the boundary between Harewood Grange and the manor of Beeley. Around Beeley are boundary stones marked with the initials of the boundaries they abut (e.g. M + B, Manor of Baslow and D D, Darley Dale). The main settlement was probably where it is now, sheltered from the hills and above the brook. Recent archaeological excavations have found flint tools on the valley floor indicating the existence of dwellers. A charter between Warner de Beeleigh and the Monks of Beauchief Abbey defines one of the boundaries of Harewood Grange (to the north) as Hareward Street. This is considered by some to be a Roman High Road although it may have been a trading route rather than a military road running along the gritstone edges.

Beeley had three open fields in the medieval period. Vanessa S. Doe in her paper "*The Common Fields of Beeley in the 11th century*" writes, "…most of the closes were held and cultivated in severalty. This process seems to have been both the consequence and the cause of increased prosperity." By the end of the 17th century all the open fields and common pastures in Beeley were enclosed as part of the process whereby the system of communal exploitation and regulation of the arable land, open pastures, meadows and wastes was replaced by a system of private land management. In the north of the country the enclosure movement was conducted largely by private agreement between manorial lords and their tenants before the Enclosure Act came in to force. Nearly all the village green near the church was enclosed and the villages had their common ground, used for recreation and animal grazing, taken away. There was much rebuilding and improved housing taking place well into the 18th century suggesting that there was industry combined with an expanding agricultural economy.

The Senior Survey (1617) of Chatsworth and its environs shows that only 80 acres of land in Beeley belonged to the Cavendish family and it was the 4th Duke of Devonshire, during his improvements to Chatsworth Park, who brought the village of Beeley into his domain as his agents purchased land and dwellings. Census returns over the centuries have shown that although farming was the major occupation, Chatsworth was the greatest employer of people. The general shape and appearance of the village of Beeley has altered very little for at least two centuries. In the 17th century the township of Beeley covered over 3,000 acres, of which more than two-thirds was moorland waste. The cultivated lands were in the valley bottom and spread up the slopes of Beeley Brook. The village was sited away from the Derwent as it periodically flooded violently and washed away the pastures along its banks. The villagers did erect earth walls along Beeley Brook during the summers when the water level was lower to help prevent flooding in the village. A map by Peter Perez Burdett based on a survey carried out in the five years between 1762 and 1767, shows it as it is today with two village streets converging to run eastward as a narrow lane. This peters out into a footpath that goes up to Hell Bank on Beeley Moor. Another street, called Pig Lane because it contained a group of pigsties, that were converted into part of a dwelling in the 1980s, now runs out behind the houses but once con-tinued east of the present road to cross the river at One Arch Bridge when it was newly built in 1761. Before the completion of the bridge it would have been the road to Chatsworth House on the east of the river and formed part of the high road from Matlock. Many of the old barns along this lane have been converted to dwellings. The road which enters the village from Chesterfield via Beeley Moor by the Devonshire Arms was made early in the 19th century. Prior to this it entered the village further up the river where there are the remains of a single arch pedestrian bridge. Pack horses would not have entered the village, they would have been left in an oval enclosure outside the village to rest overnight so that they could get over the steep hill to Chesterfield the following day.

Above: Chapel Hill, early 1900s

Along the "new" road are a group of modern houses that were built as council houses; the earliest being built between the wars with the latest in the 1960s. Maybe these are the houses built as a result of the meeting in Beeley in May 1919 when the question of housing and sanitation was considered. Reverend Chadwick who was residing said that the conditions in the village were deplorable and if it were "dumped down in the East End London ... it would be regarded as a slum parish." There was overcrowding and in the summer, a shortage of fresh water. The meeting decided to build six new houses and bring the attention of the water system to the District Council.

Beeley c.1950 (right). Until 1925 the old shed with the corrugated iron roof was the workshop of Mr H Buckley (Wood's Foreman). He was a talented joiner. With increased age Mr Buckley became quite crippled with arthritis and he used two wooden stakes as walking sticks. He would cajole the children of the village to fetch him $1/2$d worth of cigarettes from George Bond who also cut the villagers' hair. The building to the left was the mortuary. On the hill, known as Hodkin's Hill, is the Old Hall. (Parts of the village became known by the names of long standing residents.) Behind the Old Hall, to the east, is a crooked barn.

The Old Hall is thought to have been the manor house of Beeley until 1559 when the manor was sold to John Greaves, aged 20, described as a yeoman, for £90 13s 4d. His family took their name from the house they lived in, now known as Beeley Hill Top Farm. Greaves House then became the manor house. It must have been re-built in the lifetime of John Greaves as the arms of King James I are set in the mantelpiece in a bedroom, formerly a drawing room. In 1613 John Greaves was also in possession of the manors of Rowsley, Gratton, Stanton, Birchover and Winster. He was buried in Beeley Church in 1621, aged 82. His memorial is a black marble flagstone on the floor of the tower. His son, also John, was one of the first trustees of Lady Manners School in 1638. The Greaves were faithful to the House of Stuart and their support of the Royal Cause impoverished them, forcing the sale of the house. George Savile of Bakewell, son of the Duke of Rutland's steward, purchased the house, but not the manor, in 1667 and he changed the name to Hill Top. The manor was subsequently purchased twenty years later from the Duke of Rutland by his nephew, George. He in turn left it to his nephew, John Gilbert Cooper of Locko who sold the estate in 12 lots to the families of Norman, Brown and Wright. The manor house thus became a farmhouse in the 17th century and was bought by the 3rd Duke of Devonshire in 1747.

The building (right) is an imposing 17th century T shaped house with a commanding position on the hillside. East side and courtyard.

Above: Beeley Hill Top south-west side.

Right: Beeley Hill Top west side.
These three 1920s photographs are
reproduced by permission of the
Derbyshire Archaeological Society.

This photograph, taken in April 1972 shows the early
17th century Old Hall. It is two and a half storeys
high with a porch on the first. The windows are
mullioned, some with cross bars. In the bedrooms
the dividing walls are single wooden boards
affording little privacy of noise from adjoining
rooms.

Charles Dickens spent time in the 1860s at the
Old Hall as a guest of the wife of the author,
Augustus Mayhew, who lived there. She painted a
watercolour of him in the walled garden with three
ladies. Outside the garden wall the village street is a
bustle of rural activity. This painting is part of the
collection at Hardwick Hall.

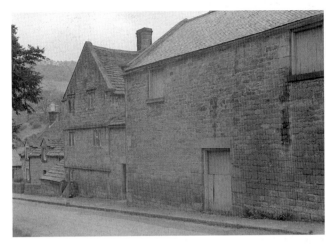

In the 1650s the Norman family had a lead smelting mill in Smelting Mill Wood between Beeley and Rowsley and a tan yard on Beeley Brook in the village. They operated small coal pits on Beeley Moor as well as gritstone quarries which supplied stone for Chatsworth. Their other quarries below Fallange Edge were the source of the lighter coloured stone for the buildings in Beeley village. Grindstones were still being made in these quarries as late as 1887. Norman House, an early 17th century house and possibly the oldest house in the village, was the home to this family who also owned outlying farms at Fallange. They continued to live in the house until early in the 19th century, a period of about 300 years.

A purpose built cheese house at Norman House has a boiling range and a shallow stone sink; the upper storey was used for storing the finished cheeses. Outside is a press of two gritstone blocks in a wooden frame. The presses were lifted by a threaded iron rod and a wing-nut. On the south wall is a bench used for draining and drying the cheeses. In the yard is a well for the supply of water. (The Old Hall has a similar cheese house at the rear.)

The house is unusual as the gable end is onto the road. This is typical of a medieval building when road space was valuable. In the 16th and 17th centuries houses faced onto the road as a display of wealth. This property has a stone spiral staircase and a newel post running almost the full height of the building.

The stones leaning against the window were put there to stop cattle banging into it. There is now another window to the right of this where the kitchen is. On the second and third storeys there are windows that were bricked up during the time of window taxes.

The rear of Norman House, (above) known at Hodkin's Yard, in the 1970s.

In the yard behind Norman House there is a circular horse walk to provide power to drive the crushing and chopping machinery for cereal production, housed in the barn adjoining the house. The machinery was later powered by petrol, diesel and ultimately, electricity. William Hodkin who lived in Norman House in the 1860s was a provider miller. He went on to take over running the corn mill (Paine's Mill) in Chatsworth Park. He ended his days at Bridge Farm in 1899. His grandson, Albert, continued farming from Norman House until he retired in 1960. William's diary of 1865-66 (edited by T.A. Burdekin) was published in 2003. It provides a fascinating insight of life in that period; a typical entry reads:

"Saturday 27th January 1866
Wm. fetched 4 score stakes and 3 bunches binding out of Northwood Car; then he went to Baslow Mill with 3 qrs oats, went to brickyard for 200 bricks to make 3 goose coats. Took the black horse to Chesterfield fair but did not sell him, a very fine day, Mrs Drabble hath lost 13 cows." [There was an outbreak of rinderpest, a virulent cattle disease, and movement of cattle was restricted.]

The barns at the far end almost go onto Chapel Hill, the furthest of which housed cattle. In 1935/6 there was an outbreak of anthrax and all the cows had to be destroyed. A pit was dug near Chapel Hill in which the cows were put and covered in lime.
The barn was converted in 1974 for Rushton's pottery downstairs with a flat above.
Just along the road from Norman House is a property called Pynot Cottage (below). It was given this name when Hugo Read moved into it in 1973. A pynot is an old name for a magpie.

The two photographs above show the frontage of the house before (1972) and after alteration (1973). The doorway has become a window and access has been created in the lower building. The chimney has been moved from the centre of the building to the lower gable end.

Right: The rear of Pynot Cottage when it was called Buckley's Yard.

This photograph above shows a property, currently called "The Wendy House", in April 1972 shortly before it was converted back to one house for Derek Hill. His father Herbert lived in one half; he in turn had succeeded his father Robert Hill, a labourer for the Building Department in 1924, living in this house. The Hill family lived in the furthest house, the nearer one being occupied by Mr Thurston, whose wife's parents lived at Park Farm. The building has 17th century features and it can be seen where the roof has been alerted by the position of the knees. The house was originally built as one with a traditional layout where entry would be through a central door opposite the chimney. It was once occupied by the vicar and then by Edward (Teddy) Fearn, Farm Bailiff for the 7th Duke, who farmed the land behind the Duke's Barn.

Further up Brookside is the Club Yard, an area that has never been owned by Chatsworth. The houses used to be owned by the Odd Fellows Manchester Unity Friendly Society and rented out. As the properties became vacant the society sold them and they are now all privately owned. The modern bungalow, out of shot on the right, was built on a patch of ground belonging to the club that Mr Hutchinson gardened. According to Beeley residents it was a beautiful garden accessed by some steps from Mr Hutchinson's farmhouse or the longer way round the lane and through a ginnel. These three houses at the top of the yard are late nineteenth century.

The house at the entrance to the yard harks back to the medieval times. The present occupants of the house found a stone spiral staircase, which had been boarded up. The window ledge has the stone carved to accommodate the curve. The layout of the house is very early. A window sill has been moulded in the 17th century from an old bit of stone that may have been an ancient road sign.

The house in the distance, beyond Club Yard, may have started out as a squatters house during the intake of land. It would have been a small cottage with an adjoining cow byre and loft above. Before the enclosures the moorland would have been used as distant grazing and animals would have moved freely.

This photograph shows Thatched Cottage off Pig Lane. The lady standing is Charles Roose's Aunt Francis who lived in the cottage. Charles was born in Beeley and a few years later the family moved to Edensor. Both his father and grandfather were gardeners at Chatsworth; his uncle, a keeper, lived at Calton Lees. Charles also worked at Chatsworth all his life.

Mrs Hutchinson, who later lived in the house with her family, cooked their meals on an open fire. One evening whilst cooking supper her son looked to be falling out of his crib and as she lunged towards him she knocked over the pan in which she was frying chips. Nothing seemed to be amiss as the child was unharmed but later that evening a neighbour alerted them as the thatch was on fire. Unbeknown to them the chimney had caught fire and the rafters going into the chimney-breast had carried the fire to the roof. The thatch was then replaced by tiles, c.1942.

The Hawksworths and the Hutchinsons traditionally lived next door to each other in cottages off the Green. In 1793 the pump of their shared well became broken. It was repaired by Broomheads of Bakewell at a cost of £6 and the expense was shared by both families. The older of the two properties fell into disrepair and Chatsworth agreed to build Church View for the Hawksworth family. The first child born in the house was in 1863; the family continued to live there until 1985 when the last elderly lady died.

This area of the village was always known as "Top of Town" hence the rhyme children used to chant:

Bottom o' village for beauty,
Top o' town for wit.
On Moor End for ugly mugs,
And up Pig Lane for ****.

The Barn was built as stabling for the 5th Duke's shire horses, and it also housed carthorses and drays which provided transport for the farm and estate. It was later used for cattle with a milking parlour and slaughterhouse. Many years ago (well before 1935/6) there was an outbreak of anthrax at Hodkin's farm (Norman House) across the road. One of the cows from the Duke's Barn herd had to be slaughtered "to save its life". This meat was butchered and taken to Chesterfield to be sold. The old boy who had taken the meat fell ill on the way home at Eastmoor and it was realised that he had anthrax. This caused quite a scare in Chesterfield.

At the rear of the barn is a shed that housed a traction engine that took ice to Cromford Canal and the return load was coal. (When the railway came to Rowsley in 1839, coal was also brought from there.) The engine was also used to take damsons to Drabbles, Dye Works in Tansley.

When Bert Reeve used the Duke's Barn the storms of 1962 blew all the blue slate tiles off the long roof. Prior to the recent conversion the courtyard was laid with two inch red granite cobbles.

Just behind the bush on the right were two stone troughs which had been brought from one of Norman House barns in the 1970s. The smaller trough was laid upside down by the side of the larger one which was positioned by the wall. Milk churns were heaved onto the lower trough then rolled onto the higher one. Eight or nine churns of milk could stand on wooden planking covering the trough to await collection by the milk wagon at the right height of the lorry bed.

These photographs were taken in October 1983.

The Duke's Yard decorated for the Golden Jubilee Celebrations for Queen Victoria in 1887. The banner over the Duke's Barn arch reads: "Long Live our Duke", with no mention of a Duchess. By the time of the Diamond Jubilee in 1897 there was a Duchess (Louise, the 8th Duke's wife) hence the assumption that this undated photograph records the Golden Jubilee as the 7th Duke was a widower.

The building on the right is the school, which was built in 1841 for the younger children; the older ones went to Edensor School. It is a low building with flat pointed arched doorways and windows with a minute belfry. In 1871 there were 93 children in the village under 14. The school closed in 1968 and has now been converted into two bungalows. The children were transferred to Pilsley School.

The school bell was originally in the Chancel of the Church and dates back to 1670. It hung in the centre of the roof (as can be seen in this photograph) and was returned to the church when the school was converted. In 1882 a Captain Phipps was staying at the Old Hall, and after complaining about the ringing of the bell, he took the law into his own hands and cut the rope. Consequently the children playing in the meadow didn't return to school on time.

This marquee was erected in the field through the arch for the Golden Jubilee Celebrations.

In May 1987 the 11th Duke of Devonshire opened a residential study centre at the Duke's Barn. The Very Reverend R. Beddoes, priest in charge of Beeley and Edensor, was the inspiration behind this development. The 11th Duke generously gave the building and a large playing field to the Royal School for the Deaf, Derby, on a free tenure for many years. The school raised £200,000 to restore and fit out the barn as a countryside centre for the deaf and other young people with disabilities to develop an understanding of the countryside. In 2001 the Royal School for the Deaf ceased to run the centre and it is now funded and run as an independent charity and is called the Ron Beddoes Outdoor Centre. All schools (and other groups) have the opportunity to use the centre for outdoor pursuits.

BEELEY CHURCH OF ENGLAND SCHOOL

Miss Clarke and pupils in 1892.

In 1874 it cost 1$\frac{1}{2}$d per week for a child to attend the school. Before the *Education Act, 1870* was passed the 7th Duke provided and maintained the school and also paid the teachers salaries. When Miss Clarke left to get married Miss Leah Ratcliffe succeeded her. In 1888 there was an outbreak of diphtheria and the drains from the Duke's yard that passed under the school were blamed. According to the school log book two children died. Other entries in the log book record that in 1878 several girls were absent from school as they had been sent by their mothers to invite trip people to tea in their homes. Also two boys were absent all week as they were employed in begging from the trip people. Visitors to Chatsworth could travel by train and alight at Rowsley Station where they would travel through Beeley.

Staff and pupils at the school in c.1910. Miss Leah Ratcliffe, headmistress is seated with Miss Evans standing behind. Among the children are ones with surnames that have been in Beeley for generations; Frances Grafton and Alice Bond (back row fourth and fifth from left); 2nd row starting third from left Lois Bond, Edith Hulley, Nellie Hutchinson, Millie Bond, Grace Fearn, Muriel Hulley, Eileen Hulley and Evelyn Hutchinson; 4th row sitting from 2nd from left Charlie Stone, Jack Bond, Sam Bond, Rollin Hawksworth and Rose Hutchinson.

THE CHURCH

The Norman church dates to about 1150. A font, which is no longer used and was cast out to gather rain-water in 1858, is thought to be pre-Norman which suggests that there was a church in Beeley in Saxon times.

In 1538 Cromwell introduced a parish register system whereby incumbents were ordered to record every baptism, marriage and burial, and a parish chest with two locks was provided. It was not until 1558 that Queen Elizabeth I ordered that the registers be kept on parchment rather than loose sheets of paper and that all old registers be transcribed. Therefore many of the 1538 registers became lost, as the transcriptions did not take place. Beeley's is one of only five Derbyshire registers to have remained.

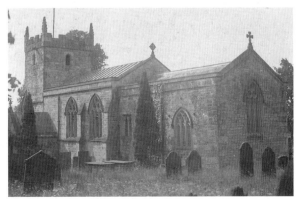

In 1819 the nave was rebuilt and the Norman pillars with early English arches were removed. The nave was rebuilt again in 1883 when the north aisle was added in a style to match the east and west arches. The large window on the south side of the chancel was reconstructed, but the Norman south doorway has survived the restoration. Pevsner considers that the restoration by H. Cockbain in 1882-4, costing £2,500, was over done. In the church there are memorial windows to the 7th Duke of Devonshire and to Lord Edward Cavendish, his third son, and there are monuments to the Savilles.

At wedding services tradition and superstition demands that the bride and groom must not approach by the west gate and must pay coinage to leave by the narrower east gate, the wider one being used for funerals. In 1785 one lady died on her way to be married.

Beeley was originally a Chapelry of Bakewell. The living was purchased in 1764 by the Duke of Devonshire and was united with Baslow. This arrangement continued until 1852. Now Beeley and Edensor are ministered by the priest in charge, who resides in Edensor.

The interior of St. Anne's Church (right). The paraffin lamps were replaced by acetylene gas. The work was completed for the first Sunday in December 1906 under the direction of the vicar Reverend Thatcher, who resigned to go to British Columbia in 1911.

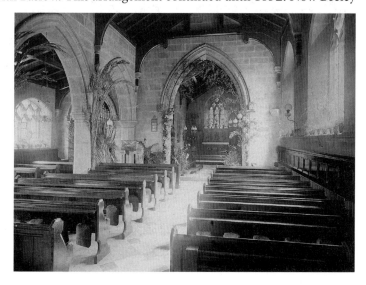

The copper beech in the centre far distance, behind the wall and picket fence, was planted on Saturday July 19th 1919 on the occasion of the Peace Celebrations after the Great War. The tree is known as the Peace Tree.

The church car park used to be an orchard. In the wall at the top is the remains of a bee bowl. A wicker-work skip would be positioned by the wall for a hive of bees to use that would gather nectar from the orchard trees.

On an April evening in 1977 the Duchess of Devonshire planted a flowering cherry tree in the Churchyard to commemorate the Queen's Silver Jubilee. That evening the villagers were all assembled in readiness for the tree planting but there was no Duchess. After a telephone call to Chatsworth the Duchess arrived a little while later, having hastily thrown on an overcoat, as the ceremony had completely slipped her mind. She hooted with laughter at her socks when I showed her this photograph.

The same evening the Duchess also planted a Jubilee tree in the grounds of the Village Hall.

On the left: Myra Critchlow, Dennis Hopkins, ?, Diana Alsop, Jacquelin Thompson, Mavis Parker, Cath Parker, Janet Culimore & child, ?, Joan Parker, Sandra Gregory, Lily Grindey, Bill Grindey, 2 children, ?, Maud Fearn, Bernard Godwin, ?, ?, Mrs Towndrow.

Opposite the village hall is Evans Corner, so named because Miss Evans (the school teacher) occupied the house on the bend called the Reading Room. Until the late 1950s the Baslow Doctors, Evans (no relation) and Alexander, used Miss Evans front room for a weekly surgery. This building, dating back to the late 17th century, was formerly the priest's house. It belonged to the vicar until 1904 when the 8th Duke of Devonshire purchased it. It was then used as a reading room until the village hall was built in 1924. The story goes that the womenfolk of the village wanted to build a stone hall but the men got the chance of some timber and hurriedly built the hall. The hall has recently been re-furbished and is available to hire for functions.

Paxton's son in law, G.H. Stokes, designed a new vicarage in 1856 in an ecclesiastical gothic style for £1,200. In 1961 it was called Dorset House but is now known again as the Vicarage.

METHODIST CHAPEL

The Wesleyan Methodist Chapel was erected in 1806 at a cost of £95. At that time Beeley church was neglecting the parishioners. From 1778 to 1852 the minister resided in Baslow and served three parishes. Beeley had only one service on a Sunday, either in the morning or afternoon, never in the evening and Holy Communion once a quarter. If there was going to be a service in the morning the parishioners were warned by hearing a bell at 8 a.m. Sometimes there was no service at all. Some of the more spiritually minded parishioners were glad for the Wesleyan preachers to come and hold evening services and prayer meetings, and so the Chapel was built. A plot of land was purchased from farmer William Brown for 10 shillings. The Chapel had boxed-in pews and buttoned doors. For anniversaries the villagers would bring their own instruments otherwise a choir member would "raise" the tune for the hymns. The building was of single stone and in 1890 was considered unsafe and pulled down.

The first chapel erected in 1806

In 1891 it was re-built, this time costing £912. The new Chapel has two reminders of the first; the date plaque put in the Sunday School (the gabled end on the left), and stone from the previous Chapel forms the basement wall. The 7th Duke of Devonshire gave the additional land required for a larger Chapel. The architect was Mr N Johnson of Whaley Bridge; the contractor Mr W Toft and the joiner Mr E Evans were both from Youlgreave.

The newly re-built chapel on Chapel Hill

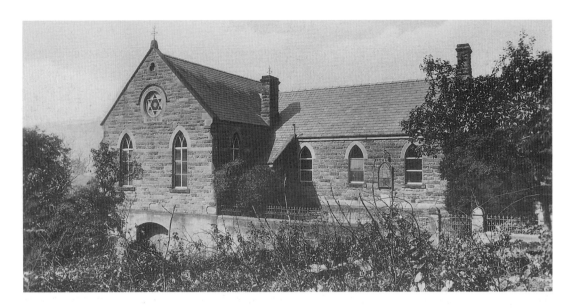

The foundation stones of the building were sponsored and the donors have their names inscribed on the stones. The heaviest corner of the building (to the left of the arch beneath the windows of the Sunday School) is supported by several stone cheese presses. In the basement there was stabling for the preacher's horse, it was later used as a fuel store and during the war a fire engine was housed there.

The Chapel seated 120 while the adjoining Sunday School could become an extension by raising a roller shutter. Extra space could be achieved by the removal of a sectional partition adding the vestry to the school. The Chapel was closed in 1996 and converted into a private dwelling.

Left: The chapel interior

Opposite the Chapel is Chapel Terrace, also known as Friendly Row. At first sight it appears to be a uniform row of three cottages but on closer inspection it can be seen the houses are of different periods. In the 1840s the cottage on the left was single storey, and may be medieval in origin, the middle section is 17th century and the end cottage was once cow sheds.

The area to the front of the Devonshire Arms is known as Devonshire Square. There were three inns in the village between 1755 – 64, only the Devonshire Arms remains. It is seen here c.1895.

Slightly opposite the Devonshire Arms are the three Y-shaped "Paxton" cottages fronting Devonshire Square; G.H Stokes is credited with their design. Stokes came to work at Chatsworth in the employ of Robertson and subsequently married one of Joseph Paxton's daughters. These houses were built to re-house villagers from Edensor when it was being re-developed in 1856. A house was pulled down to build these cottages and evidence has been found of a stone pavement to the old house. Although picturesque, the leaded windows make the cottages rather dark inside as the panes of glass are very small. Metal leaded windows were only used in this area after the arrival of the station at Rowsley in 1839.

The building to the right at the foot of Chapel Hill is the Smithy. The blacksmith in the 1930s was Tom Wall who came

from a family of blacksmiths; his father Samuel being one before him. They also had premises in Rowsley and Pilsley, Sam Wall living in Pilsley. Tom Wall was also the clerk to the parish council and the rate collector. Next door to him, in School House, (above the Smithy & below Chapel Terrace) lived Mrs Storer the last school headmistress. She had a fearsome re-putation and would crack children on the knuckles with the sharp side of the ruler if their handwriting was not good enough. The Smithy is now a village shop and café with a very pleasant tea-garden surrounded by herbs.

Just along the brook are Brookside Cottages (right). Note the intricate pattern on the tiled roof.

The shop was also the village post office and tea-room serving refreshments. In 1891 there were two shop keepers in the village Mrs Hannah Cocker and Mrs Rebecca Hawksworth whose husband George was the shoemaker, living and working beyond the Chapel in a property now called Last Cottage. Bassett Briggs ran the refreshment rooms. By the time of this photograph, c.1920s, Thomas Burdekin was the shopkeeper. The roof in this image is thatched albeit a close thin thatch. This was removed in 1949 when the roof level was raised by two courses and the dormer window removed.

Mr Grafton and one of his daughters outside the shop (below). The shop keeper a this time was Harry Reeve. The advertisement above the shop door is for motor hire and there is a public telephone on the premises. Overhead cables are visible between the shop and the Chapel. The shop closed in 1990.

The Holmes family were one of the few remaining free holders in the village when the 6th Duke of Devonshire was making his alterations and improvements to the properties. They built this house facing the Devonshire Arms in the mid-1840s.

   The Holmes family also built the house on the other side of the brook in the mid-1840s. This property, Brook House, was a butchers shop. The gable end is seen here on the left. Access was over a foot bridge and there was a door into the shop, which was the room where the bay window is now. After the Holmes tenure, the Ollivants were the butchers; Mrs Ollivant being a niece of the Holmes family. She was well known for her home-pressed tongues.

The building across the road from Brook House (which looks like a garage with an eight paned window) was also a butcher's shop and hooks and rails remain in it. In this image the house has bay windows which were a later addition. Behind this building was a single storey cow shed and slaughter-house. The roof was raised when it became a dwelling. This area is known as Brookside.

DEVONSHIRE ARMS

The Devonshire Arms dates from the 18th century and it is thought the building was converted from three cottages in 1747 when the farmstead opened as a coaching inn. John Holmes was the first innkeeper, until 1771. In 1841 the innkeeper was Joshua Holmes, living with his wife Elizabeth, his mother Ellen and four children. By 1851 aged 48, he had re-married to Melissa Elliott and had two more children. Like most inns, the Devonshire Arms was also run as a farm. By 1881 the widow Melissa Holmes was running the inn with her daughter and three servants, leaving in 1890. In the next 72 years the inn keepers were George Downs, John Richard and then two members of the Reeve family ran the inn for 54 years.

Below: The Devonshire Arms exterior in 1944 before the extension was added in the 1960s.

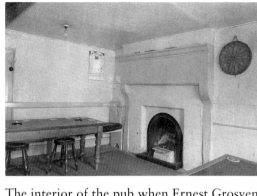

The interior of the pub when Ernest Grosvenor became the tenant in 1962.

Immediately after he took over the tenancy he refurbished the interior. Some of the fittings of the inn, carriage lamps and a huge boiling table, are from the Chatsworth Estate. Beams and flooring timbers are from Paxton's demolished Barbrook House. His son John is now the tenant of this busy public house.

On Thursday 11th July 1872 a thunderstorm caused Beeley Brook to burst its banks and flooded the square. History repeated itself on Sunday 31st August 1997. The height of the water is marked on a beam in the bar.

The building behind the pub car park is a Derbyshire Longhouse over 300 years old. A longhouse was a barn and dwelling under one roof with a cross passage between them.

The water from Beeley Brook was harnessed to provide power for a corn mill. The mill was on the right just beyond the bridge in this photograph. In later years this became a tannery run by the Norman family. Where the brook curved the water was drawn off and there were tan pits for washing the skins. Slightly higher up the brook was a long bridge with a pig house on top – making mucking out really easy! Sadly it was taken down in the 1920s when a storm washed a tree stump into it making it unsafe.

Above: On Beeley meadow across the road from the square the local men (and youths) would play football. This photograph (above) of c.1905 shows the team; from left, standing: ?, S. Halowes, C. Buckley, S. Grafton, kneeling: G. Burdkin, R. Morton, E. Morton and sitting G. Hawksworth, W. Gilbert, F. Wagstaff, T. Stone and G. Buckley.

Right: In this early 1930s photograph are G. Bowering, Ted Bond, Charlie Roose, Geoff Bond and Billie Roose.

In 1994 Frank Robinson was involved in the discovery of evidence of a bronze age cremation burial on the flood plain of the River Derwent. The find was west of Beeley on the eastern bank of the river near the meadow. The excavations uncovered cremated bones within a collared urn accompanied by a copper alloy dagger knife, which was purposefully placed there. Other finds produced artefacts to suggest that this part of the valley had been used over the pre-historic and historic periods. The material also includes evidence of medieval cultivation.

In 1955 there was a consolidation of land holding in Beeley, this being part of the re-organisation of the Chatsworth Estates after the death of the 10th Duke of Devonshire and the imposition of 80% death duties. At this time there were 17 land holding tenants. When two of the older farmers decided to retire it meant that a new tenant could be found for Hill Top Farm and the house could be modernised. This happened in 1960. During the previous decade Hill Top was barely fit for habitation as the roof

was falling in, and the farm buildings were also generally unsafe. In 1969, when milking premises had to be improved to new hygienic standards, a large modern timber barn was built utilising some of the old building walls for use as a dairy.

Until the mid-20th century there were eight or nine farms or small holdings in the village. Most had a couple of cows which would be taken to graze in Chatsworth Park. Only a few farmers had sufficient land to enable them to bring the cows home for milking, the other owners would have to travel to milk their cows. In 1953 the Robinson family started farming in Beeley from a small barn at the top of Brookside, the family living elsewhere in the village. (Then eight cows were sufficient to support a family of four.) The small barn was a house in the 17th century; a wing extending at right angles no longer remains. This building could be a remnant of the dispersed village when the open field system started to break down and farms started moving out of the village.

In 1969 to the south of the village the Chatsworth Estates built a new dairy farm and house on a green field site; South Oaks Farm. The Robinson family who had slowly built up their land holding in Beeley over the previous years, by taking up tenancies when they became available, were the tenants. There now remain two main farms, Beeley Hill Top Farm and Moor Farm, as the Robinsons have now retired from farming, and Chatsworth Farms having taken most of the Robinsons land in hand. Traditionally large estates did not farm land themselves, letting the land and farms to tenant farmers. It is only in the last century that estates have started to farm commercially and taken land in hand as the farms have become vacant.

The Mill,
River & Blue Doors

The lower weir and One Arch Bridge with the river Derwent in flood in 1961. This bridge was designed by James Paine and constructed when the new road from Beeley to Edensor was formed through the Park c.1758. The span of the single arch over the river is 62 feet.

In April 1933 the *Derbyshire Times* reported an inquiry at Bakewell against an application for an order prohibiting the use of vehicles exceeding three tons from using the bridge. Several local bus companies were represented and Roland Burke was there on behalf of Chatsworth's need to "regulate traffic on the bridge on special occasions". The report quotes that "motor coach trips which include the run through Chatsworth Park were very popular especially so when it was possible to visit Chatsworth. If the bridge were closed they would have to reach Chatsworth through country which was not nearly so picturesque…". A Mr Harrison said he represented 1,300 owners of commercial vehicles and who said the run through the Park was one of the most popular in the country. It was not disputed that a restriction on the bridge was required and the County Council suggested a limit of five tons. The limit on the bridge today is 7.5 tons.

The lower weir was reconstructed in 1774 under the supervision of Joseph Pickford. Its purpose was to raise the water level in the river where the headrace took the water to the mill. The headrace is mainly underground but emerges a short distance from the mill and is joined by a small stream running from a spring. The present weir, built of millstone grit, dates from 1838 when the original one was replaced.

The mill (left) at the Beeley end of Chatsworth Park was built in 1761-2 to designs by James Paine. This was during the time of the 4th Duke's landscape improvements when the routes of roads through the park were changed and the One Arch Bridge built. This mill replaced the main estate flour mill which stood on the east bank of the river closer to Chatsworth House. It was the only new building to be built within the eighteenth century park that was designed to be both functional and pleasing to the eye. The mill had a long working life, finally being used to store animal feed until 1952.

In 1857 it is noted in *White's Gazetteer* that Henry Strutt the corn miller lived at Bridge House. George Hodkin was miller in the 1930s.

In 1962 storms brought down two large beech trees, which demolished the roof and part of the mill. Rather than demolish the ruin it was decided to make it safe. A good view of it can be seen from the end of the Canal Pond in Chatsworth garden where it completes the long vista.

The Mill as it can be seen today. This image dates from the 1970s.

One Arch Bridge with smoke coming from the chimney of "South Lodge", a small gate house adjoining the farm. The occupant looked after this gate at the southern edge of the Park. The building is now all one dwelling known as Bridge Farm.

Under the bridge is a grille that was constructed in 1884 to prevent livestock and the deer escaping down stream.

Over the bridge towards Beeley is another gate house called Blue Doors (previously Beeley Lodge). Wyatville designed a pair of lodges for the Beeley end of the Park but died in 1840 before this single one was built. This house was probably designed by Stokes, the son-in-law of Joseph Paxton. In the Chatsworth accounts of 1855 there is a record of a payment of £577 for the construction of "New Lodge, Beeley".

This entrance to Chatsworth goes through the Old Park where there are ancient oak trees. It has always been said that the Old Park used to be part of Sherwood Forest in the time of Robin Hood, but John Barnatt and Tom Williamson have now disproved this in their book *Chatsworth a Landscape History*.

This postcard was sent to Mrs Roose, Beeley Lodge, nr. Rowsley from Lindup, Cobden Road, Chesterfield with the question: "What do you think of the new postcard?" signed W.

Calton Lees

In medieval documents of 1205, Calton Lees was first referred to as "Lees" and a place called "Calton" was recorded in 1192, but this may have been Calton Pastures where there are earthwork remains of a medieval settlement. Calton Lees is a small hamlet that would have been passed through on one of the early roads to Edensor. Later, the 6th Duke of Devonshire made a "Green Drive", a recreational route for guests and visitors to view the Park. The scenic drive left the public road between Edensor

and One Arch Bridge; it climbed the hill to the south-west of Chatsworth and zigzagged to Calton Pasture before returning to the Park through Calton Lees.

On the edge of Calton Pastures is the Russian Cottage (below). Tsar Nicolas I was a friend of the 6th Duke and he sent the Duke a model of a Russian village from which this design was taken. The single storey building is X-shaped, built in 1855 of timber beneath a steeply pitched roof.

These images are 1940s (top) and 1969 (bottom).

The road from Calton Lees, bottom right, leads up to Calton Houses and on to Calton Pasture. The road up the hill peters out, but was once one of the 6th Dukes circular 'Green Drives'.

Calton Lees House (below) when the garden was formally planted in terraces, probably in the 1930s.

Above: Calton Lees House in the 1980s.

Below: Calton Lees in 1954. Mr Wilfred Grafton, a security man at Chatsworth, lived in the left side of the pair of houses on the right of this photograph. When I came to work at the Sawmill (in Calton Lees) in 1984, his sons Fred and Tom still lived there with their sister Melissa.

Mr Roose, the Keeper, lived in the house on the right and when Harold MacMillan visited Chatsworth he would visit Mr Roose and sit chatting outside the house.

THE SAWMILL

Trees are a crop and large estates always have sawmills as part of the harvesting process; Chatsworth is no exception. The woods have been managed since the mid-1700s. When Frith was Head Forester in the late 1800s he had 100 men planting trees. During the First World War hundreds of acres of trees were felled, but these and new plantations were re-planted.

Below: In 1958; Derek Neave riding pillion on Harold Birkett's motorbike at Calton Lees Sawmill. The crane in the background was used to hoist the tree trunks into position for sawing. Although the crane functioned perfectly well, it was condemned by the Health and Safety Executive in the late 1980s and had to be dismantled. Up until ten years ago the timber was still manually rolled through an opening on the top right side of the building on to a rack bench. It was sawn by a 6 foot circular saw with inserted teeth. To aid lubrication, and also to act as a coolant, diesel was thrown onto the blade. All the sawdust generated collected in a huge pit beneath the saw and bench which had to be dug out and barrowed away by hand.

The Sawmill yard is now used as warehousing for the successful Chatsworth Farm Shop. The circular saw and rack bench have found a new home in Bolsover.

Above: Jack Shaw with his timber wagon in the late 1950s.

Below: Jack Shaw on the lorry with Woodbine Willy (Billy Harrison) standing on the far left.

Cyril Neale, John Hill and David Allinson, forestry workers, in the early 1960s at the sawmill.

Forestry workers at Edensor Nursery c.1960s. Left to right; Len Newton, Jeff Hamilton, Jim Whiteman, Bryan Bonsall, John Heathcote, unknown, and Brian Gilbert. The tree nursery was established in 1961 and millions of seedlings were grown for planting on the estate. The Nursery is at the top of Edensor village and the buildings there (which were once racing stables) are now used as a base for the Forestry Department. There was a nursery at Calton Lees where the Garden Centre is and another nursery at the top of High Street in Pilsley. In the mid 1950s this was lined out with trees which have now grown and formed a plantation.

Colin Hopkins (right), forestry worker, in the early 1970s.

Sawmill workers (middle) in 1910. 2nd from the left W. Grindey, 7th, J. Blackwell, 11th, G. Hilson and 13th, C. Buckley.

Sawmill staff (bottom) and their tools of the trade in the summer of 1987. From the left: David Rimmer who operated the Bobcat tree felling machine, David Jones and Paul Oliver with their tractors that had cranes, winches and timber trailers fitted, Colin Cother, lorry driver, Bryan Bonsall and Tom Grafton, foresters, Geoff Machin, Head Forester, myself, Gordon Pearce, Assistant Head Forester, Mark Adams and John Mann, sawmill workers and Peter Halse sawmill foreman.

The long timber clad building behind the office housed a Tanalising plant in which harvested and milled timber was pressure treated to extend its life.

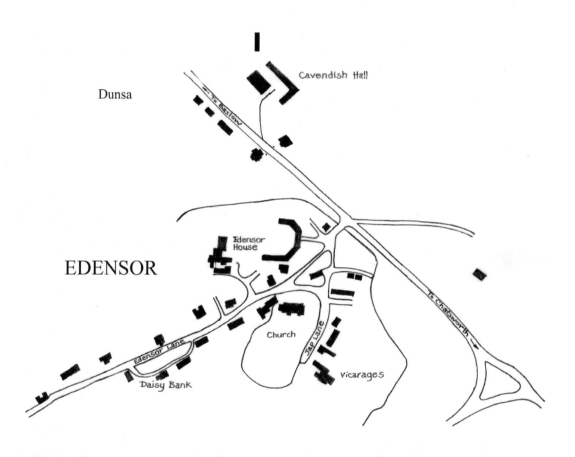

Dunsa

Cavendish Hall

EDENSOR

To Baslow

Edensor House

To Chatsworth

Church

Jap Lane

Edensor Lane

Daisy Bank

Vicarages

EDENSOR

To understand why the model estate village is seen as it is today it is necessary to know a little of its history. The Saxon name for the village was Ednesoure. It was an important place in pre-Norman times as there was a moat court (place and field names of Moatless remain). Ednesoure was in the Wapentake an administrative division of the High Peak and courts were held here and at Youlgreave. It is recorded in the Domesday Book when it was owned by Henry de Ferrers. Through marriages and changes of fortune the manor became the property of Sir William Cavendish in 1549 in whose family it has remained. Until the 1760s it sprawled on both sides of the road to the west of the Derwent and much of it was in the ownership of the people who lived there; it was predominantly a farming community.

The 4th Duke of Devonshire during his tenure made extensive improvements to the landscape and setting of Chatsworth House. His intention was to clear the park of buildings that were visible from the west front of the House, but he died in 1764 before this could be completed (which it was in the late-1770s by the 5th Duke). One of his most notable changes was the alteration of the road pattern and changing the course of the river. In this he was aided by Capability Brown whose involvement at Chatsworth started in 1757. The old Edensor Bridge and Mill were lost and a new road was constructed on the west bank of the Derwent, which had been straightened out. The river was crossed by the new One Arch Bridge at the Beeley end of the Park, designed by James Paine, the architect. The road went up a steep climb by the side of the new mill, through the park and eventually down a steep decline where the traffic entered the village via Jap Lane. The High Street of the village now passed the new Park Gates where a new coaching inn was built in 1779 to meet the need of travellers using the new coach-road from Matlock to Baslow. The turnpike, created in 1739, ran from Bakewell to Chesterfield via Edensor. The 5th Duke, as a trustee, was involved in the creation of turnpikes all over the county and had other inns on turnpike roads; for example Newhaven House and the Eagle (Buxton) on the Buxton to Ashbourne turnpike. The 5th Duke removed the remaining few houses and the vicarage that straggled over the flat ground in front of the House.

The 6th Duke of Devonshire continued the improvements to the village. In the 1810s and 1820s he made land purchases and re-aligned the roads. His new road through the park on the approach to Chatsworth House no longer passed through the village. This meant that part of the village had to be lost and by 1831 he had demolished the lower and eastern parts of the village, and the cottagers were re-housed in new houses in Pilsley and Beeley. One house of this part of the village remains in the Park enclosed by a stone wall. During dry weather the route of the old High Street and house foundations can be seen. It is now generally accepted that it was Paxton who saw the possibility of making Edensor a "model village", re-modelling the existing properties and enclosing the village. The Chatsworth accounts of 1833 show that payments were made for new gardens, garden walls and gates, and for the widening of the road. In 1838 J. Robertson was paid for designing ten cottages and shortly after work commenced on improvements to these and the building of new ones. A total of thirteen houses dating from 1785 or earlier were re-modelled by Paxton and new houses were built from locally quarried buff coloured stone.

Paxton was aided in his re-building and alterations by Robertson who joined the staff in 1841 and remained in the Duke's employment for three years. He was an architectural draughtsman and had been employed since 1829 by John Cornelius Loudon, the gardener and landscape architect. Paxton knew Loudon and probably met Robertson when visiting Loudon's premises in Bayswater. The 6th Duke notes in his *Handbook to Chatsworth* of 1844: "The village of Edensor was new-modelled and rebuilt between 1839 and 1841". The old Edensor was a ragged conglomeration of non-descript buildings unworthy of a well run estate. This new modelling was not purely for aesthetic reasons, although it was a show piece of architectural innovation. From the 1830s there was increasing concern amongst landowners for the physical and moral well being of their workers. The 6th Duke had improved staff accommodation at Chatsworth House with the building of the new wing and he extended this to his workforce in the villages by providing them with new dwellings.

The major significant alteration to the village after the 6th Duke's death in 1858 was the re-building of St. Peter's Church (below & following page top). Then, early in the twentieth century a group of four houses, Teapot Row, was added opposite the Cavendish Hall and Moor View House, at the top of Edensor Lane, built probably to designs by W.H. Romaine-Walker. The other development was the conversion of barns and outbuildings at the back of Edensor House into a bungalow for the Duchess's groom, Angela Napier in the 1970s. This is called Burke's bungalow after Sir Rowland Burke, Agent from c.1920 to1939. The listing of the buildings and land did not take place until 1967 whereby any changes now have to be approved by the appropriate authorities. In 1989, the vicar, Reverend Ron Beddowes, formerly Provost of Derby Cathedral, and a well-respected and much loved man, said of Edensor "in our present state [it is] almost an oasis of civilisation".

The houses of Teapot Row (above). These houses were so named owing to the copious quantities of tea drunk by the builders, Cox Wilson. In the foreground is the bowling green that is now completely enclosed by the beech hedge that is just getting established in this photograph of 1971.

The 5th Duke of Devonshire bought land from the Cowley family in 1798. The freehold included the Talbot Inn, together with an orchard of almost three acres and a small croft with adjoining stable. The purchase of this land allowed the Duke to widen the road going north out of the village. (The line of the road, B6012, is now northwest.)

The new modelling of the Talbot Inn by Paxton in 1838-49 created a house in a Swiss chalet style. The main walls belong to the old 18th century building and the large roof was designed to overhang a balcony which originally encircled the whole of the first floor. Now there is just a small balcony left at the front, on which a fir tree is placed at Christmas lit with fairy lights.

The house is now called "The Italian Villa", strange for a Swiss chalet styled house!

Aerial view (right) showing the group of buildings:-

Italian Villa and Park View (left), the post office, tearooms and cottage (right).

Below: Italian Villa is on the far left and to the right is the fountain that was built to a design of Robertson's in 1841, on the site of the Talbot Inn yard and brewhouse. It hides the back of the farmhouse.

Park View (right) stands next door to the Italian Villa overlooking the green. The front and roof of the house were part of Paxton's re-modelling but the rear was not touched. In the 1960s the 18th century structure at the back of the house collapsed and was replaced with slate covered walls and metal windows. Nowadays the authorities would insist that the style of the original structure be retained.

In 1821 the 6th Duke of Devonshire purchased the Lees freehold. This enabled him to enlarge the Park by the addition of fields behind Daisy Bank and also the Great and Little Crofts (this land is know known as the Crobbs and stretches up the hill east from the village towards Chatsworth and the edge of the golf course.) By 1826 the Duke completed the purchase of the Lees freehold from Richard Lees' sister Mary Gilley by buying the farmhouse and adjoining cottage (below).

The farmhouse, which was a substantial size, is now the Post Office and Tearooms, and the Post Office Cottage.

The gable end of the Lees original farmhouse had a small wing added onto the back of it when it was divided to make two dwellings. Both the gabled end and the wing have been given the Paxton treatment with a stone capped roof and pinnacles. At one time there was a stone staircase leading to the large room under the gable, which suggests it may once have been a shop.

Above: The outbuildings to the farmhouse have been sympathetically converted into a tearoom and garaging for the villagers' cars. All overhead cables (telephone and electricity) were put underground in the early 1990s to enhance the appearance of the village.

Recently the newspaper delivery lorry drove into the stone arch at 4 a.m. demolishing it. The sound had people up and out of their beds thinking there had been a gas explosion. The driver was a little shaken and it was amusing to meet our neighbours clad in their night attire in the early hours of the morning. Our next door neighbours who live right next door to the arch never heard a thing!

Edensor Tea Rooms interior in 1967.

The Gatehouse is by the cattle grid at the entrance to the enclosed village. This castellated lodge was designed by Robertson and was once the post office. The entrance was on the left. The stone gatepost on the right was moved so that the entrance could widened when a cattle grid and access gate were added. The path on the left in front of the gatehouse is no more, a shrub, *rhus glabra*, grows in its place, but the iron railings outside the village remain.

Aerial view of the gatehouse (right), 1995, showing the widened gateway to accommodate the cattle grid, which over the years became worn. Metal plates were fitted over the bars to make it safe and a few wiley sheep and lambs learnt how to negotiate the grid. They became nightly visitors to the village, grazing flowers in the gardens that are not protected by walls, until it was mended.

The School House (below) is almost certainly designed by Robertson and dates from 1841, though Paxton may have had some say in the choice of style. It is well sited in the new village landscape on the edge of the green facing the site of the school. In the 1950s Mr Wilkins, who lived at School House, took in students who were working on the estate. After the school was demolished laburnum trees were planted around the green and these were replaced with crab apple trees in 1984. The crab apples provide a useful autumn's equivalent to the snowball when students are waiting for the bus to take them to Lady Manners' School.

It is known that in 1785 the present vicarage was not owned by the estate, but by Philip Melton, yet the date the estate acquired the freehold is uncertain. There is evidence on other parts of the estate that when the freehold was acquired re-building and alterations were done. Since the front of the building was re-built to stand six feet away from the pavement in 1836 (shown on maps) it is possible that the freehold could therefore have been purchased sometime in the first 30 years of the 19th century. The style of the house is a Georgian box with a rear wing. The wing houses the kitchen and has been extended several times. The last time it was extended was in 1920 when a nursery was built over the wood shed for the children of the new agent, Gerry Hartopp. He later moved to Barbrook (Paxton's house) and the librarian, Francis Thompson, took up residence. It became the vicarage in 1973 when the existing Old Vicarage was divided into two.

Above: This Vicarage is in the centre of this photograph of 1995, Nos 1 & 2 Old Vicarage are on the right. The ha ha surrounding the east side of the village can be clearly seen here.

The Vicarage (overleaf) was the principal house in the village in the 18th century and was shown as such on the O.S. map of the village dated 1878. Reverend Joseph Hall was the incumbent from 1856 until 1907 and lived at the Vicarage at this time. Paxton's re-modelling of the village refers to "the parsonage" without stating which building it is. The parsonage on Unwin's map of 1831 had been demolished by the time Paxton re-modelled the village, so it is not sure if the reference is to this Vicarage or another building. The map of 1878 shows a doubling in length of the kitchen wing to the north, the demolition of the east wing and the building of a new wing which contained the vicar's study. From 1858 the accounts do not reflect the expenditure on the Vicarage so Hugo Read, Chatsworth Agent 1955 – 1973, assumes what he had been told to be true; that Reverend Joseph Hall was a wealthy vicar with a large family and he did the re-building at his own expense.

In 1973 the house was divided into two and the vicar's study, with doors opening onto the garden, became the sitting room for the smaller house. These images show the building before it was made into two dwellings now called 1 & 2 Old Vicarage.

The date and origin of Tower House (above) is unknown. It is built on what was the garden and orchard of the Lees farmhouse (now post office) bought in 1821. Plans show that it was definitely built before Robertson designed his encircling stepped stone wall in 1841. There is no designer credited with the design of the house and the construction looks as if it was built in two stages with the southern section being an afterthought. On this photograph the long window in the centre of the building, which is there now, appears to be a stone recess.

These three cottages were built in a gothic style at a cost of £1,050 in 1868 at the time the church was re-built. The saying goes that they were built on the site of the building yard for the church

with surplus stone. The two outer cottages are mirror images of each other with a smaller cottage in between. Note the height of the chimneys in the older of the two photographs.

Mr & Mrs Carnelly, who lived in the top cottage until the mid-1990s, grew, and sold plants at the end of their path in aid of church funds. They had previously lived at Calton Houses and were avid gardeners.

Below: The bottom of Jap Lane from the Green, 1969.

The Chatsworth Building Accounts of 1844 record a payment of £1,116 to a John Vickers for building the Gamekeepers House (above). This was the last year Robertson worked at Edensor before going back to London. On Robertson's map it is called Blockley House and it is now known as Norman House. When Dennis Fisher occupied this house he painted murals on the bathroom walls imitating the cyclamen that Lucian Freud painted on the Sabine bathroom walls at Chatsworth House.

The house has a commanding position in the village. The back drive to Edensor House can be seen on the right in front of Norman House.

Most of the houses on the right side as you go up Edensor Lane were newly built rather than existing houses updated. All houses were built purely for the external appearances and consequently many of them have an abundance of little rooms quite unsuitable for today's demands.

Above: Norman House is a pair of cottages with an unusual shared porch, Rose Cottage and Sunnybank (left), giving them the appearance of one house. These cottages look as if they were originally very small but substantial extensions have been built on to the rear of each.

Rock Villa bears the date it was built, 1839. This photograph (left) was taken in 1967.

In the 1950s the Misses Bacon ran the village shop. When they left the shop they moved to Rock Villa where they took in students as lodgers.

The next dwelling going up the lane is Bank Top. The bungalow was a new building built in the 1830s on rising ground above the lane out of the village going west to Bakewell. It had offices built adjoining the property which are now garages and outbuildings.

Moor View (above) is quite untypical of other buildings in the village as it does not conform to the Paxton treatment, being of a later date, but nevertheless it fits perfectly in a village where there is no consistency in style. It is typical of a house of its period, built in 1912 in an Arts and Crafts style. It was designed by the architect Romaine Walker and was built by the builders Cox Wilson. It is similar in style to other houses they built such as Redway Farm. The house was initially occupied by F.R. Barnes the Surveyor of Buildings and on Lady Day in 1926 John George Weston, Head Gardener, left a smaller cottage in the village to move there.

At the top of the village is a tardis-like gate-house (right), i.e. it appears tiny from the outside and is quite roomy inside. This is another of the new houses built by Paxton, now known as Top Cottage. J. Tilbrook, an under-keeper, occupied it in the early 1920s and Thomas Tucker moved there in 1926.

Note the size of the chimneys in this 1967 photograph; quite out of proportion to the size of the house. This stack had to be re-built a couple of years ago.

The house (above), now known as Barbrook Cottage, was originally two separate buildings. In 1801 Constable did a pen and wash drawing of Edensor (which is in the Victoria and Albert Museum) and the two houses stand in the foreground. By 1838 the larger roadside building had been demolished and Paxton added an extra bay to the smaller building facing down the hill. He built over the stream culvert leaving a trap door in the floor, and in 1964 the open culvert was replaced by a pipe. In the heavy downpour in 2000 this could not cope with the deluge and it overflowed. This and several other houses in the village were flooded.

Moor View has not been built in this photograph of early 1900.

Below: This photograph shows how the new extension at the rear of Barbrook Cottage neatly blends in with the older building. Mr William Shimwell was the new occupant. He was comptroller from 1921 – 1950 and became clerk of works for the estate until he retired in 1964, aged 69.

When the next family moved into the house they unearthed a well in the garden that had previously been filled with garden waste and rubble and then forgotten about over the years. Once all the debris had been removed a wooden hatch with a ring in it was found. When this was opened up it was discovered that there were steps leading into an underground brick lined

cavern where the well is. The valley beyond this house has a multitude of springs and soughs rising to the surface, but this well is not connected with the sough that runs beneath the house.

Dated 11th March 1967 after the completion of the extension built by four generations of the Sellars family. On the left is Malcolm Sellars (with the 11th Duke and Duchess), his father Walter, his son Jack and his grandson Malcolm. The dog is Danny who ran free at shoots, burying the fallen birds.

Coming back down the lane on the other side are the houses and bungalow on Daisy Bank. The houses had new façades built onto the old back walls and new roofs. To the far left of the houses is a building with a stone cross on the wall; this is known as the mortuary. The path into the Park goes up the left side of the mortuary.

Daisy Bank.
Note the middle photograph shows much taller chimneys than those on the lower photograph.

Similarly the other two old houses on this side of Edensor Lane were given new façades with much decoration in varying styles. One is now called Shepherd's Cottage and the other remains un-named. In between these two cottages outbuildings are neatly hidden behind a fancy stone wall.

The (stone) string course around the rendered Shepherd's Cottage, on the right of the photograph above, is in fact painted timber.

Shepherd's Cottage (right), the ornate front to the out-buildings and the un-named cottage (centre).

Behind the house called Deerlands (the garden is immediately on the right of this photograph) there are steps going up onto flat ground where there was a common drying ground and laundry was hung out to dry. To preserve the idea of a model village the washing had to be dried out of sight and vegetable gardens and pig-sties were also not allowed to be seen. The allotments for the villagers were at the top of the village with buildings for livestock. A path went from the drying ground round the back of houses next to it and met with the steps that enter the village from the Park past the "Mortuary".

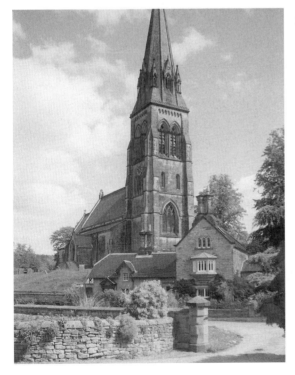

Above: Guide Cottage (right) and Church View (left), with Edensor School on the Green, c1930.

The two cottages in the shadow of the church are further dwarfed as the church is built on higher ground thus adding to its height and size.

The smaller of the two cottages is now known as Guide Cottage due to the fact that Mrs Joyce Fisher used it as the Girl Guides' meeting room in the 1960s.

65

The backs of the two cottages suffered from damp and had to be re-built in the 1970s. The occupants of one of the houses were "temporarily" re-housed in the bungalow on Daisy Bank where they have remained as they liked it so much.

Above: Church View, on the right, and Guide Cottage frame the vista up Edensor Lane. Both were older buildings that were re-modelled by Paxton.

Left: Church View c.1970

Edensor Boys School dated from 1841. The old school was demolished together with the adjoining cottage and workshop before the school seen here could be built on the same site. The design is attributed to Robertson and is typical of several village schools in Loudon's encyclopaedia of pure Italian style. The main school was roughly a cube with a low-pitched roof. There was a porch at the east end and the roof had two belfries. At the west end there was a wall concealing a yard in which the fuel store and toilets were located.

The last school-master was Mr Wragg who lived in School House. He is noted for teaching the boys to write in copperplate. Mr Wragg was also the organist at the church and the father of Tom Wragg, first Assistant and then Librarian at Chatsworth for 40 years until his death in 1978. The school was demolished in 1950, as the building was no longer required. The stone was used to build the first pair of the Hartington Memorial cottages in Pilsley that same year.

Below: Seen in this image is a wall around the Cavendish flats (on the right) that has since been removed and there is a door and flight of steps to the cottage adjoining the post office (on the left) that is also no longer there.

I wonder if the work that is taking place on the green and church steps is in preparation for Lady Rachel Cavendish's wedding in August 1923 when flag-poles and bunting were put up?

Above: An early photograph of the school showing the chimney on the east end, which was later taken down.

Below: Pupils at Edensor Boys School, 1890

Above: This later image of the school, taken shortly before it was demolished, clearly shows the Italian influence. The chimney at the east end is no longer standing

Below: A weeping beech stands on the site of the school and the school name in stone is on the grass in front of it.

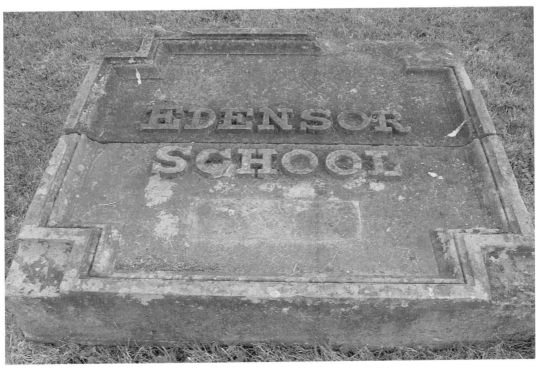

It was the 7th Duke of Devonshire who altered the fourteenth century church. His great-uncle the 6th Duke had spared it when the village was re-modelled. The 7th Duke was a deeply religious man who decided that the old church was not worthy of Edensor and its place in the village and estate. He invited Sir George Gilbert Scott to enlarge it. Scott was at the height of his career having just won a competition to design the Home and Foreign Office in Whitehall. He also designed the Albert Memorial in London and the hotel and station at St. Pancras. The work on the church was completed in 1868 and the new church was consecrated in 1870. The church spire is 166 feet high, topped by a gold cockerel which can be seen glinting above the tree tops from Chatsworth House on a sunny day.

The work on the church was not the straightforward demolition of an existing church nor the restoration and enlargement of the existing fabric but a re-building of the church. The basis of the design was taken from the existing church so that certain dimensions of the old church were respected whilst it was also enlarged. It took two years to demolish the old church and prepare the foundations trenches. It is surmised that it took this long because the Cavendish Monument had to be dismantled and stored. (The Cavendish Monument is a memorial to William, 1st Earl of Devonshire and Henry Cavendish, Bess of Hardwick's sons.) Also much of the stone from the old church was used in the re-building. The 7th Duke's agent, Cottingham, oversaw the building work whilst Mr Marriott was the main contractor. A quarry was re-opened locally to supply the stone for the new church. Throughout the year of 1867 the new church rose from its foundations whilst other work was

70

undertaken in the churchyard and further churchyard walls were built. (Paxton had surrounded part of the old churchyard with a new wall and gateway in 1844.) Twigg & Co. were paid for the work to the stone sedilia, pulpit and font. The sedilia, a fine example of the quality of stone carving employed throughout the church, was used as a seat for the clergy during services. Twiggs were also paid for "restoring the monuments" which would include the re-erecting of the Cavendish Monument in the new Cavendish Chapel. The total cost of the re-building of Edensor Church is given as £13,741. For the time this is a very large figure which reflects the craftsmanship and materials used on the church.

Right: Edensor Church c.1860. Photograph by Garner, 23 Buxton Road, Stockport.

The old church had a single west tower with single belfry openings and a weathervane at its centre. There were four bells, one of which, dated 1669, hangs over the Stable Block at Chatsworth. The other three were re-cast in 1867 and form part of the six bells that are in the new tower.

Reproduced by kind permission of Mr R. Hubbuck, Hampshire.

The tomb in the foreground is that of Sir Joseph Paxton who died 8th June 1865. Members of his family are also buried in this tomb. This photograph can therefore be dated between 1865 and 1866 when the re-building of the church commenced. The railings around the grave were probably removed in 1940 as part of the war effort.

The cottage on the right side is shown on the 1785 map of Edensor but is no longer there. It shows evidence of having been given the Paxton treatment by the detail on the barge boards on the gable end and the tile-hung walls. This cottage was probably demolished around the time of the church re-building as it is not on the 1878 Ordnance Survey map, and the row of three cottages built on its site. A Captain Barker is recorded as living in a house on this site. The trees on the skyline are much more dense today.

Above: The church porch has largely been re-built in the same style as the Norman original and the semi circular stone arch above the door is from the earlier church. The patterning shows a distinctive chevron, a common feature of Norman architecture.

Below: The church font is supported by a column of grey crinoidal marble from Sheldon which is surrounded by four pillars of a marble called "The Duke's Red" due to its colour. The seam from which this marble was dug has been exhausted. A font cover, made by Ray Bradshaw and gilded by Lawrence Udall, was unveiled in 1993.

A little seen view of the church from the garden of Edensor House.

Below: The Cavendish family burial plot is at the top of the churchyard. In the foreground is the grave of Lord Frederick Cavendish. In 1882, as a Liberal MP, he was appointed Chief Secretary for Ireland and duly went there. Within twelve hours of his arrival in Dublin he was murdered in Phoenix Park, May 1882. His murder caused a public outcry. A wreath of everlasting flowers sent by Queen Victoria, at the time of his funeral, hangs in the church chapel.

Lord Frederick's wife Lucy Caroline (d.1925) is now buried with him. The stone surround and small arched headstone, seen here, have been replaced by a Celtic cross.

Behind this grave is the tomb of William Spencer Cavendish, 6th Duke of Devonshire.

Buried in the family plot is Kathleen Kennedy who was married to the 10th Duke's eldest son, William, Marquess of Hartington. He was killed in action in September 1944 and is buried in a military cemetery in Belgium. She died in a plane crash four years later. A stone in front of her grave records the visit of her brother, President Kennedy in 1963. This photograph is when her youngest brother Senator Edward Kennedy and his wife Joan visited the grave in May 1965. On the right is the 11th Duke of Devonshire.

The sundial in the churchyard sits on a column five feet high, rising from four square stone steps which are 30" high. The sundial is more decorative than practical – unless the viewer is on horseback! Joyce Critchlow in her book *Derbyshire Churchyards* believes that the column was originally the shaft of an ancient cross.

The wedding of Lady Rachel Cavendish to Lord James Stuart of Findhorn (later Viscount), 4th August 1923.

The bride is arriving at St Peter's Church, Edensor with her father the 9th Duke of Devonshire. On the left onlookers are sitting on the wall surrounding the now demolished Edensor Boys School.

The married couple leaving the church down the north steps. The girl in white with her arm outstretched and long hair is Joyce Fisher (neé Burdekin) aged 11 years. When she was 16 she went on to be a nanny to David Stuart one of Rachel's children who was born in 1924. She later married Dennis Fisher the House Comptroller.

Annually there used to be a village day held in Edensor on St Peter's Day where there was a fête and a display of local crafts in the church. In the 1920s a long table would be set up on the village green and everybody joined together in afternoon tea where a much more frugal fare than we see today would have been served. Afterwards there would be sports at the bottom of the Crobbs since there was very little traffic on the road, which both adults and children would join in.

Above left: Spectators watching the sports in front of Edensor in the 1940s. Above right: 1940s ladies tug of war team. To the left is Sid Child. The lodge cottages can be seen in the distance on both of these photographs.

Sports on St Peter's Day 1972: left to right children: Andrew Oliver, Lisa Taylor (and her mother Linda) and Joanne Gilbert; adults: standing: Linda and Brian Gilbert, Rita and Bryan Bonsall, John Oliver and Cliff Gilbert, ?.

Above left: This display in 1967 is commemorating one hundred years since the re-building of the church.

Above right, below left & right: In 1995 work was carried out on the steeple. When the work was complete a new weathervane in the form of a golden cockerel was put in place at the top of the steeple. Pilsley Village school children attended the ceremony when Reverend Beddowes blessed the golden cockerel before it was mounted high above. Among the children are Julie Shimwell, Alex Slater, Christopher Dore, and at the front Jake Hill and Justine Storey, accompanied by their Headmistress, Ann Hall.

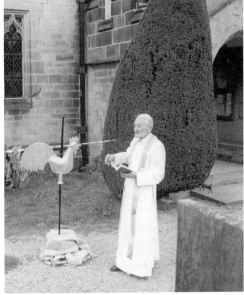

Above: When Reverend Beddowes retired Michael Gowdey was licensed as the new Vicar at Edensor on 23rd July 1997. Reverend Gowdey is the closest in the third row from the left. Behind him are Ian Fisher, Kath Bosett, Denis Hopkins and Hugh Blakey, church wardens, followed by the Diocesan Registrar, the Archdeacon of Chesterfield (David Garnet) and the Bishop of Derby.

Below: This photograph was taken after the blessing of the Millennium tree that was planted in the churchyard. Left to right; Reverend Michael Gowdey, 11th Duke of Devonshire, Rob Dowding, the present Dowager Duchess of Devonshire, the Very Reverend Ron Beddoes, Vernon Mather (Reader), the Bishop of Derby and Canon Bob Honner. (Canon Honner was the vicar of Edensor before Rev. Ron Beddoes.) The yew tree was propagated from ancient yews estimated to be 2,000 years old by the Conservation Foundation. About 7,000 Millennium yews were distributed to parishes throughout the country and Rob had collected the Edensor yew tree from Derby Cathedral.

EDENSOR HOUSE

Edensor House was originally a single storey farmhouse. It was designed, along with what are now the Cavendish Flats, by Decimus Burton in 1836. The house was approached through an arch in the farm buildings through a large yard protected by the U design of the buildings. The arms of the U were 200 feet long. The house functioned as a farmhouse until 1853 when the bailiff Benjamin Swafield left. After the 6th Duke's death in 1858 this group of buildings was altered and the house enlarged with the addition of a second storey to make what is now Edensor House. The ends of the long U arms were demolished and a new drive was built to the side of the gatehouse. These alterations were for the new agent; John Gregory Cottingham. The agent Gilson Martin then lived in Edensor House, until his death in 1908, and was succeeded by John Pepys Cockrell. Sir Roland Burke continued the tradition of the agents living at Edensor House until the 1940s. In the 1920s he held a large ball and all the teenage girls in the village were allowed to go to watch the guests arrive. He had his own private staff and in the archives of Chatsworth House it is recorded that his staff lived in cottages in the village. Sir Roland Burke was knighted for his work for the Royal Agricultural Society of England. (At that time the Royal Show toured the country.) In the time of Sir Roland Burke there were four agents under him who looked after the outlying estates. This system continued until there was a change in policy in the 1940s after the 10th Duke had succeeded in 1938.

The 11th Duke and Duchess of Devonshire moved into Edensor House in 1947 and lived there until 1959 when they moved into Chatsworth House.

Above: Edensor House and gardens.

Right: The U shaped Cavendish flats and School House with Church View bottom left.

The farm buildings continued to be used and housed draught horses until 1910 when they were converted to the estate office. The horses moved to the newly built Stud Farm at Pilsley. The offices had previously been in buildings adjoining Edensor House, which are now the cottage of Edensor House. Changes are afoot again as Edensor House is currently being divided to make two dwellings.

When the estate office moved from the stables to the Edensor Inn in 1958, they were converted to the Cavendish Flats. Some are purposely designed for the retired Chatsworth workers and have stair lifts installed, others are occupied by younger single people.

Right: On the reverse is written: "Mr and Mrs Martin pleased to wish you and yours a happy xmas 1906". There is every possibility therefore that the couple sitting on the lawn are Mr and Mrs Gilson Martin, as it was customary for people to send cards illustrating themselves.

It is therefore likely that the couple at the far end of the conservatory (below) are Mr and Mrs Martin. The elderly lady surrounded by people gathered for tennis and croquet, could be a widowed Mrs Martin and her family in later years. Sadly the person who lent me these images could not identify the people in them.

Above: The garden of Edensor House. The lines of a tennis court are marked out on the grass.

Left and bottom left: The interior of Edensor House decorated in Victorian times. On the wall in the hall hangs a portrait of the 7th Duke.
Bottom right: The staff of Edensor House, early 1900s.

Park Cottage is the only house to remain on the old High Street. The house on the site today was built in the early 19th century but a house is shown on this site on a map dated c.1785. It stands alone and is enclosed by a stone wall. There is no documentary evidence to say why this house was not demolished with the rest of the houses on the High Street but it is said that the 6th Duke did not demolish it as part of his re-modelling of Edensor because the occupant was elderly and he did not want to move him.

Below: It looks as if the enclosing garden wall had not been built at the time of this photograph.

At one time afternoon teas were served at the cottage as can be seen by the notice on the front door.

Below: Tudor Lodge and The Lodge with the Cavendish Hall behind the trees, at the Edensor end of the Park.

The Park Lodge Houses: the house on the left is called Tudor Lodge and is in the style of an Old English Lodge, the one on the right is Italian in style simply called the Lodge. Both houses were designed by Jeffry Wyaville and built in 1837. Robertson was so taken by the style of them that he sent plans and drawings of their design to Loudon who subsequently printed them in his 2nd edition of *Encyclopaedia of Cottage Farm and Villa Architecture*, 1846. It was the intention that two similar lodges were to be built at the Beeley end of the Park but this was never carried out.

During the 1920s and into the '30s Rolls Royce used the road through the Park for trails, running just the chassis (and engine).

Until the council took over the maintenance of the road the gates at both ends of the Park were locked at 10pm nightly. Note the absence of a cattle grid.

Park Rangers' House behind the Cavendish Hall (below) was originally built as two lodges with a drive-through archway in between them. When the newly routed road skirted the village it may have passed under the archway. Although it is thought that this route was intended as a shortcut for people on horseback or foot, no formal drive ever ran in to the Park from there. It is possible

therefore that Paine may have designed these houses as part of his work for the 4th Duke. An alternative is that they could have been designed by Joseph Pickford at the time he was working on the Edensor Inn. The mason, Hawksworth, who was working on the inn helped with a lodge which could be these buildings. When the gatehouse was no longer required the archway was filled in sometime in the nineteenth century to make a detached building.

Mr Burke (as he was then) met a Mr Joseph Jackson at a Royal Show, he invited Mr Jackson to join the Chatsworth staff as Clerk of Works and he subsequently moved to Edensor with his family in 1922. At that time heads of department were given the larger properties and it was expected that daughters would stay at home to run the house. Mr Jackson moved to Park Rangers' House (then it was known at Park Lodge) after the Head Forester, Mr Robertson vacated it.

When Hugo Read came to Chatsworth in 1955 the house had not been modernised and in 1960 it was renovated. When the work was taking place evidence was found of the two lodges and arch. On the photograph it can be seen where a pair of round-headed windows have replaced where the wooden porch was. The entrance to the house is now entirely from the other (eastern) side.

Inside the house are stone spiral staircases that can only be reached from the second floor due to the alterations, and the cellars have to be accessed from outside the building.

CAVENDISH HALL/ESTATE OFFICE

The 5th Duke commissioned Joseph Pickford of Derby to design the Edensor Inn. It was built of red brick in 1776-7. The bricks were burned in the park in specially constructed kilns from brick earth that was dug in the park. The old inn that stood by the park gates had developed an unfavourable reputation amongst travellers and was demolished. The site for the new inn was several hundred yards outside the park beyond the park gates. It has the appearance more of a gentleman's club than an ale house. The entry in Glover's *Guide to Derbyshire*, 1830, reads:

"Edensor Inn was built by the late Duke of Devonshire, for the accommodation of travellers. It is a comfortable Inn, situate a short distance from the village church, upon the verge of Chatsworth park, and near to the lodge. It is built of stone and has a handsome portico. In the open area in front of the house grows a beautiful oak tree. Mr Walters, the present occupier, keeps excellent post chaises and horses; and every accommodation and attention is paid by him and his family to those parties who visit his house."

Right: The inn was initially rendered and had the appearance of stone; the oak tree is still there.

When the 6th Duke made his alterations to the village this building was spared and enhanced the new carriage-way. In 1827 the inn was enlarged with the addition of a 2-storey kitchen and a staff block, probably to accommodate the extra visitors to see the progress of the new wing at Chatsworth House. A floor plan of 1910 shows 12 letting bedrooms and stabling for 40 horses. Mrs Harrison kept the inn in the 1920s, she is remembered as sitting behind her counter with a mop cap covering her hair.

Below: The building with the bay window housed the kitchen wing. This was demolished when a ballroom was added to the north side early in the twentieth century when the Edensor Hotel became the Institute. It can be seen on the far left of these images. It was at this time that the rendering was removed to expose the brickwork and stone string course that is seen today. A second billiard room was constructed above the coffee room and behind the hall there was new accommodation for single men, plus communal bathing facilities.

Every Saturday night in the 1920s the "big room" at the Institute was used as a cinema to show silent movies. The projector was housed in a small projection room accessed from a staircase

outside the building. During the Second World War the Home Guard were based at the Institute and they used the old projection room as their base, where they would sleep when on duty. On a Friday night they would go on manoeuvres under the direction of Sergeant Roose. The men would march around the area and have a pint of beer at the Devonshire Arms in Pilsley before returning to base. The unfortunate soldiers who lived in Pilsley then had to walk home again.

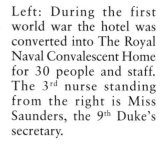

Left: During the first world war the hotel was converted into The Royal Naval Convalescent Home for 30 people and staff. The 3rd nurse standing from the right is Miss Saunders, the 9th Duke's secretary.

At Christmas in 1917 the sailors decorated the Recreation Hall with bunting and tinsel for the Children's Party. 250 children were entertained by a conjuror and ventriloquist and tea was served with the sailors acting as waiters. The children were all given presents by Father Christmas and the hospital staff were given gifts by Mrs Cockrell, the Agent's wife.

In 1958 the southern side of the institute was converted to the estate office leaving the institute with five rooms plus a flat for the steward. The coffee room is now the main accounts office. Part of the Stables and outbuildings were rebuilt as a Bothy of four rooms in 1967. Then in 1971 women were first admitted as members of the institute. This necessitated a few minor alterations including the building of new toilets.

A petrol station was set up at the Estate Office in the early 1960s when the closure of the garage at Baslow was imminent due to the building work being carried out at the Devonshire Arms Hotel. Three underground tanks were installed with brass pumps, one gallon at a time being

Right: Aerial photograph showing Tudor Lodge and the Lodge in the foreground with the Cavendish Hall and Park Rangers House behind Tea Pot Row is on the left.

delivered, with a maximum of ten before the pump had to be reset. The building housing the pumps used to be a canteen for the hospital during the war after which it was converted to a joiners shop. When the swimming pool was built the diesel tank was used to store heating oil for the pool then in 1996 the tanks were taken out of use.

Below: When the swimming pool was built, in 1973-4, the bricks had to be specially made so that they were the same size to match the bricks of the main building. In addition to the swimming pool, a tennis room, and bowls and golf stores were built on the site of some of the original stables and sheds. In 1999 outbuildings were converted to a gymnasium and beauty salon.

Annually an Estate Staff Party is held in March. The first "Party and Dance" was in 1958 when a printed programme laid out the dances and entertainment for the evening. Grosvenor Catering provided the buffet at 3s/6d.

Above: Staff and guests in 1963 at the Cavendish Hall (it was known as the Institute). Among the men on the left at the front are Derek Neave, John Holmes, Peter Childs, Keith Wilkins, David Morton, a Baslow policeman plus Mrs Morton. Nowadays the dress is more informal and there is no ballroom dancing, instead a disco.

A collection of Hugo Read's ex-pupils met Heads of Department outside the Estate Office in the mid 1960s.

left to right: Dennis Fisher (Comptroller), Bert Link (Head Gardener), Bob Starling (Farms Manager, he went on to become Agent for the Duke of Grafton), Derrick Penrose (Deputy Agent and later Agent), Fred Bond, Ollie Carr (Agent at Wentworth), ?, Jack Eaton (Owner of Mapledurham, Reading (which was used in the film *The Eagle Has Landed*), ?, Roger Carr (Agent for Moray Estates in Scotland, which was owned by the Stuarts of Findhorn; the 9th Duke's daughter Rachel married into this family), Christopher Harewood (New College, Oxford), Tom Wragg (Librarian), ?, Jack Newton (Inland Revenue), Willie Shimwell (Head of Building De-partment), Giles T. Sampson (Accountant), Tom Lord (Head Keeper), Charles White (Assistant Surveyor), Tatton Hewetson, Bill Cherry (Clerk of Works), Bill Eskine (Minerals Agent) and Anthony Bryant (National Trust for Scotland). Hugo Read took the photograph.

The Chatsworth Horticultural Show is held annually at the end of the summer. All estate villagers, tenants and pensioners are given the chance to show their produce. Classes include vegetables, flowers and domestic (jam, chutney, bread, handicrafts), with special cups and prizes for different categories. Children have the chance to grow the tallest sunflower and show their handiwork. In 1964 the Duchess of Devonshire presented Mrs Dorothy Roose and Mr Jess Grafton with cups; looking on is Mrs Ruth Read (right).

At the show in August 1973 Eric Oliver, House Comptroller until 1996, received a trophy for his vegetables from Mary, Dowager Duchess of Devonshire. Looking on are Bert Link, left, and Hugo Read.

Below: Sir John Betjeman (on the left) opened the show on 26th August 1978. Next to him is Mrs Carnelly, Chairman. Mary, Dowager Duchess of Devonshire is between Mrs Carnelly and Mr G. Rippon the show's honorary secretary.

The hall is used for many and various functions. The Peak Music Society, founded by Hugo Read and now in its 38th season, has used the hall as the venue for their concerts. Many famous musicians have graced the stage over the years. It is interesting to compare the rear of the hall. In 1964 (horticulture show image) the hall had not been altered to accommodate toilets and a lobby. The back wall and balcony, which can be seen in the concert image, were part of the alterations.

Morris Dancing in the Cavendish Hall, part of St Peter's Day festivities, 29th June 1973.

When computers were introduced to the Estate in 1989 the staff training took place in the Cavendish Hall. At the front is Derrick Penrose, Agent.

Left to right: Faizal Mirza (Assistant Accountant), Nancy Chadwick (Chatsworth Food), Sheila Blackburn (Farm secretary), Victoria Edwards (Head of House Shops), Ian Else (Surveyor), Liz

Copley (Farm Shop secretary), Andrew Middlemiss (Farmyard Manager), Sandy Boyd (Farm Shop Manager), myself, Margaret Brightmore (Catering secretary) and Michael Isherwood (Accountant).

There are three of us still working at Chatsworth; Faizal, Ian and myself. Others have died, retired or moved onto other work.

DUNSA

Dunsa is a small hamlet of six houses to the north of Edensor, just beyond Teapot Row. The house on the higher ground is Dunsa Villa (now Dunsa House), built for a Miss Thornhill to designs by Paxton c.1848. There is no record of a payment for the building of this property in the estate accounts and Hugo Read assumes that the Duke must have paid for it personally. Payments for additions do appear in the accounts especially after Miss Thornhill's death, when the house was occupied by other tenants and employees; John McLauchlan, head keeper from 1905 – 1950 being one of them. Locally the house is known as one of the 6th Duke's birdcages, where he kept his lady friends.

In the early 1950s the roof required urgent repair but there was a lack of funds available following the death of the 10th Duke of Devonshire. At the same time the former inn was being converted to the estate office and the firm carrying out that work were consulted. It was suggested that a traditional stone capped shallower eave replaced the original eave that had a big overhang. Therefore the exterior of the villa is as Paxton designed it with the exception of the

roof. Later in the 1950s the interior was re-designed with an ensuite bathroom in the turret where the staircase had previously been. An elegant staircase was built in the centre of the house. Hugo Read writes in *A Century of Change*: "I like to think that if Paxton had been designing for the domestic requirements of the 1950s he would have planned his interior in the form it now takes."

Behind this pair of cottages (below), known as the Kennels, is a large range of outbuildings comprising part of Dunsa Farm. These buildings are used by the keepers. The keepers job involves the management of the deer herds in the Park and the deer larder is at Dunsa.

The Keepers House (below), a bungalow, was built in 1964 for Dick Norris. Since all the old farm outbuildings were being used by the game department it was a logical move for the Head Keeper to live at Dunsa.

Shoot Day in 1995 at Dunsa. The keepers are standing by the two cottages. Back: left to right Robert Wrath, Mick Rimmer, William Wrath, Andy Wrath, Derek Neave, Kim ? Front: left to right Paul Wrath, Paul Tooley. Andy, Derek and Paul were the keepers employed by Chatsworth and the other men were beaters. All the Wraths are brothers.

The implement shed at Dunsa in the 1970s. Dunsa is centrally located for working on the estate so the tractors are kept there. There is also a large modern building that is used to house cattle during the winter months and a lambing shed that was built in 1981.

Chicken coops at Dunsa in 1966. Left to right Harry Jones, Fred Carr and Dick Norris.

The chickens were used to rear pheasant chicks. Broody hens would sit in separate boxes on pheasant eggs. Every day the chickens would be taken off the eggs and tethered by one leg whilst they were fed and watered and then returned to the nests until the eggs hatched. When the chicks were a fortnight old they were put in a coop with the hens until they were big enough to be released.

This was the last year that chickens were used to rear the chicks as incubators were used the following year. Prior to 1964 each keeper would rear chicks on his own land; Fred Carr at Russian Cottage, Harry Jones at Swiss House in Stand Wood and Derek Neave and Twink (aka Ralph Lord) at Pilsley. After Dick Norris became Head Keeper all chicks were raised at Dunsa.

PILSLEY

The village of Pilsley lies immediately north of the B6048 and the civil parish of Pilsley is part of the ecclesiastical parish of Edensor. It is on higher ground than Edensor and has views over the Derwent valley towards the gritstone Baslow Edge to the north-east and toward the limestone Longstone Edge to the west. The Domesday Book (1086) mentions it as Pirelaie. At this time the parish of Edensor, which included Pilsley, belonged to Henry de Ferrers and later passed to the Foljambe family. By 1205, it was known as Pilisley and later Pillesleya, but by the time of the Saxton map of 1577 it was called Pilsley. Leah (ley) is the word for a clearing; Pilsley could therefore mean Pil's clearing. It is partly a planned village, but was once a single street development on an old packhorse route. New houses were built and the village was extended in the 18th century to re-house estate workers whose dwellings in the old village of Edensor had been demolished by the 4th Duke. The school at the top, the school house and other buildings around the green date from when the 6th Duke of Devonshire relocated more villagers from Edensor in the 1840s.

Out of sight of the green the High Street comes down the slope from the west and continues north-east as Pilsley Lane until it reaches the B6012. Going west past Top House the lane divides into three which all peter out into paths and tracks, Bradley Lane going north to Hassop, Sitch Lane straight ahead west, and Field Lane south towards Handley Bottom and Bakewell. Field Lane is now called Rood Lane as many fields along it are a rood in size. All three routes were probably packhorse ways, the latter being the most important as it went on to Monyash, where the road continued onto Cheshire and Staffordshire. Packhorses carrying salt and lead would travel this route. There were three ale houses and one inn on the High Street to accommodate the travellers and drovers. The horses were changed at Pilsley before going over the eastern moors. The life of a pack horse was four years, and in hilly country it could be even less. In the 1760s there was a branch road to Pilsley off the road from Edensor to Baslow. It went from Edensor, through Dunsa and entered the village past where the Farm Shop now is. On Peter

PILSLEY

c.1925

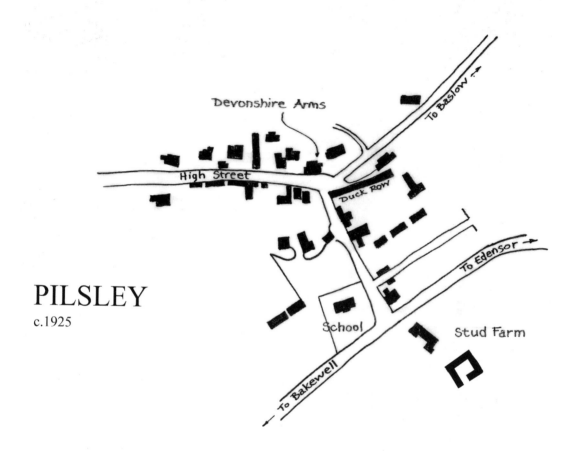

Above: High Street

Potter's map of 1805 it can be seen where the road to Bakewell forked off this on the village green and went via Ballcross. The branch road was upgraded in 1812 to form part of the Ashford to Edensor turnpike effectively bypassing the village.

Pilsley was primarily a farming community; in 1617 documents record field names of Ferney field, Oxeclose, the Railes and Thurlow. In 1662 there were 15 families living in Pilsley. Burdett's map of 1767 shows Pilsley as a tiny village with its buildings confined to the houses on Duck Row. By the time of Glover's Guide of 1830 the description is "the hamlet of Pilsley [in 1821] 43 houses, 45 families and 243 inhabitants.... Of the 45 families 30 were employed in agriculture, 9 in trade, and 6 variously." In 1850 a James Syson Nibbs (a school teacher from Baslow) invented and patented an Oxydate Condensing Lamp. He had premises in Pilsley and manufactured the lamp under the name of Nibbs & Co., Pilsley. The lamp, which used oil as the fuel, was called "Vesper" and gave a clear and uniform light for twelve hours without attention, at the rate of two hours for a farthing. It received testimonials from the *Magazine of Science*, 1851, *The Artizan*, June, 1851 and the Society of Arts Exhibition, Adelphi, London.

Below: Many of the houses on the right going up the High Street were once small-holdings with strips of land at their rear.

Unwin's map of 1836 shows that the 6th Duke of Devonshire had started buying properties in the village and taking the land in hand. The layout of the village was pretty much as it is today after the 6th Duke and Paxton had made their additions. There are now about sixty houses in Pilsley and all are owned by the Chatsworth Estate. As Pilsley is part of the parish of Edensor it does not have a church but it used to have a chapel on the High Street, which closed in the early 1940s.

DEVONSHIRE ARMS

The Devonshire Arms dates back to 1739. At that time Richard Harrison and his family were the tenants; they were also farmers. Until the 1950s there was a small farmyard at the back of the inn as farming was always a secondary occupation for the innkeeper, who had a smallholding of 20 acres. The main farmyard was across the road where there were cowsheds and stalls for calves; in the middle was the hay store with a hayloft over the cowshed. There were also pigsties. In 1835 there was another inn in the village, called the Snake and Crown, kept by Samuel Mather. It is reputed that there was also one called the Bunch of Grapes. But by 1849, the Devonshire Arms was the only inn and was kept by Margaret Wilson, a dealer in ale, along with her daughter-in-law and four grandchildren.

Members of the Newton family ran the Devonshire Arms from 1852 to 1937. In 1871 the innkeeper was Henry Blagden, his wife Mary being a Newton. At that time there were three rooms on the ground floor, three bedrooms, a yard, stable and cow house. A few years later the inn must have been enlarged, as there was a taproom, bar, smoke room, parlour and kitchen with six bedrooms. Outside there was a stable, cart shed and cow house. On the site of the car park there was a cottage adjoining the neighbouring farmhouse that was demolished to create parking. The cottage was latterly used by Simpson's Bakery.

Right: Johnnie Newton with Peter (the horse). Johnnie was the last innkeeper of the Newton family. During a particularly bad winter in the 1930s the village children took over Pilsley Lane for 5 to 6 weeks as it was a good sledge run from the top of the High Street all the way down Pilsley Lane to the Thatched Cottage on Baslow Lane. Mr Newton threw ashes on the ice and snow in front of the pub, which the children either cleared or sledged over. He lost one of his

legs after an accident that involved catching a runaway horse. His wife and daughter continued to run the pub until 1937. Since then there have been a succession of innkeepers, some staying just a few years and others for 20 years or more. The current innkeeper is Rod Spensley, who has kept the pub since 1994 and provides a fine carvery.

For the duration of the Second World War, George Hamilton Constantine, who was responsible for the restoration of the Painted Hall ceiling at Chatsworth in 1937-9, lodged at Edensor. He was the Technical Director of Sheffield City Art Galleries. In addition to being a talented artist, he exhibited at the Royal Academy and was a member of the Sheffield Society of Artists. In 1940 he arranged for a large proportion of the picture stock from the Sheffield Art Galleries to be taken to Pilsley for safety during the war. The paintings were stored in the back room of the Devonshire Arms.

When Richard Howard was innkeeper (1937 – 57), his daughter recollects, the door of the pub was always open when the pub was open for business. In the 1930s Mr Howard had been a policeman in India. The inn was mainly for the use of men and no food was served. The bar didn't extend into the tap room although there was a serving hatch which was rarely used. Instead, service was rung for and the drinks were carried through, usually by Dorothy Howard. This is the same today except customers now fetch their own drinks. The beer, Offilers ale, Youngers beer from Scotland and Ind Coope was tapped in the cellar and poured either directly into glasses, or enamel jugs when it was busy. Bottled beers came from Burton on Trent (delivered) and Bass & Worthington was fetched from Ormes of Bakewell. Whittaker's minerals (soft drinks) came from Matlock Bath. The spirit licence was granted in 1958 when Herbert Armstrong took over.

Left: Forestry workers celebrating the retirement of Billy Jones in 1975/6. Left to right: Len Newton, Peter Enion, John Hughes (Head Forester), David Robinson, Billy Jones, Maurice Fearn, Bryan Bonsall, Walter Hancock, David Sidwell and Brian Gilbert.

BAKERY

Slightly opposite the Devonshire Arms is the Post Office and village shop. This was also the bakery until 1962. The advert states that "G.S. [George Siddons] has baked Chatsworth Bread since 1894". It shows dole bread being distributed by the bakery at Christmas. A map of 1924 shows that the Siddons were still the bakers. Bread was delivered by horse and trap to local shops and for home delivery.

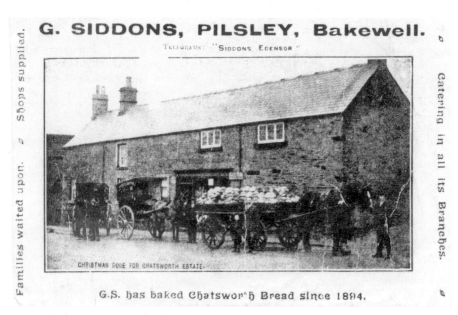

The next baker, Mr Garfoot, combined his bread-making with being a Wesleyan Minister. He eventually gave up baking in favour of the latter. In 1935 George Simpson arrived from Horncastle to take over the bakery and he combined running the bakery with, more appropriately, the post office and village store. Running the bakery was a family affair, his wife, grandfather and son helping, with the assistance of other staff.

Left: Gordon Bowering on his bicycle outside the bakery under the ownership of G.H. Simpson in the 1930s. On the wall is a timetable for North Western buses with the post box next to it. Gordon was killed in the Second World War, and his namesake lent me this photograph.

Above: The bake house stuck out 14 feet at the back of the building with two ovens and a stoke hole. (The bake house no longer remains.) Three barrows of coke was enough for one days fuel supply for the ovens with a maximum temperature of 450 degrees Fahrenheit being reached. Once a year the fire was cooled off to enable the tubes to be checked that carried the steam to heat the ovens. Upstairs in the bake house was the motor that ran the dough mixing machine. Before the war the two-stroke machine was changed to electricity and when it was running the floor would bounce. Chatsworth was informed and they put a metal railway line rail (with a date of 1861 on in) through the building to strengthen it.

Daily the dough mixing machine would get through 25 stone of flour (plus water) to make 240 loaves, the maximum amount of 2lb tins to fill both ovens. In addition to bread the bakery made all manner of cakes and pastries and on a Saturday Mr Simpson's son Ken would go round with a hand cart and take the fancies from door to door. The boys from the village would wait by the loading window and surreptitiously pinch buns when nobody was looking. (The loading window was down the alley and can be seen blanked out in this photograph.) At Christmas, 4lb Dundee slabcakes were made, approximately 150 a day. Daily before the war Cliff College was supplied with 4lb sandwich loaves and 30 to 40 loaves were delivered each day to the Still Room at Chatsworth House. Mr Simpson baked the bread for the Penrhos College school girls who were evacuated to Chatsworth House during the war and his daily delivery increased. Also deliveries were made to the farms and neighbouring villages by van. The loft doors where the flour was hoisted by crane into the building remain in this 1974 photograph.

Right: The bakery today with the loft windows removed and the original window restored. The loading window has also been opened up. To continue the baking theme the lane alongside the shop is called Bun Alley. At the end of the alley are sheds where carriages were originally kept, in which the Simpson's later kept their vans and Ken kept his motorbike.

The eight Mary Devonshire Cottages facing the green were constructed in 1959 to provide additional accommodation for estate workers. At this time the offices in Chesterfield were being moved to Chatsworth and these houses were built for the office staff. The houses are named after the 10th Duke's wife. The twin terraces were built with local materials to match the architecture of the village. To enable the houses to be built economically the whole of the interior structure was made of hemlock spruce from the estate and reconstructed gritstone facing blocks were used for the outer walls. The architects were Messrs Hadfield, Cawkwell and Davidson.

On the site of the Mary Devonshire cottages were farm buildings, including a joiners shop. During the war some of the upper part of the buildings was used for the storage of food stuffs and paper for re-cycling was collected and stored on the ground floor. The yard was used for re-cycling house bricks where they were cleaned and the mortar knocked off.

The most recent building in the village is a pair of cottages near the post office called 11th Duke Bungalows, on the site of a building where gates were made. This pair of cottages was built using reclaimed industrial stone from Glossop by Sheldons builders in 1990. Opposite these cottages on the green is where the main water bore entered the village. Around the village are stone posts on to which the taps were attached. The water came by pipe from Park Gate Farm to Pilsley via the Paddocks. The pipe crossed the River Derwent on the old metal foot bridge between Hare Park and the Home Farm. This was the main supply until the bridge was washed away in December 1965. Mains water was then brought to the village.

During the course of speaking to local residents I have heard the village green variously called lumpits, lompits, long pits and long pitch and nobody can be sure why. It is rumoured that it may have something to do with lime pits but this seems unlikely, as there is no evidence of lime burning kilns on the green. On Peter Potter's 1805 map, an area, near where the road junction now is, is called Lumb Pit Close, with a pound in the field corner. Maybe this is where the name has come from?

The House to the right is Smithy House. The blacksmith, Sam Wall was the last smith in the village. There were two parts to the Smithy; the yard where park gates and wheels were made and the large room with two huge fireplaces into which the horses were taken to be shod, including those from Stud Farm. In the late 1930s the boys in the village would help by working the bellows. The smith didn't make wheels himself but he made the "tyre". He created the steel rim in the forge and bent the band in degrees until the red hot ends met. The ring was then put in a big fire on the village green. Four hefty blokes would lift the white hot rim, with long rods, onto the wooden wheel which burst into flames. It was tapped into position then picked up and dropped into the trough. The dowsing of the flame would shrink the metal onto the rim. The trough on the green was 8 to 9ft square, made from four stones butted in at the ends. There are conflicting views as to the supply of water to it. Either it was an extension of the piped water that came into the village at Duck Row or the well behind where the Mary Devonshire cottages are now fed it. Nevertheless the blacksmith had the ability to fill the trough as required, which was also used as drinking water for the stallions from the Stud Farm. During the war an army vehicle drove into the trough, damaging it, and after the war it was removed. The village green was also badly cut up by the army vehicles practicing reversing and general manoeuvres. After the war at the village meeting Fred Bond, the House Comptroller, negotiated with the War Office to have the village green re-laid and a sum of money was given towards the cost. When Stud Farm was converted to a dairy, Sam Wall's work slowly dwindled even though most farms had a horse and cart. On his retirement the Smithy was divided to make two garages. Not surprisingly lots of hand made nails still get dug up in the garden.

Right: Ted Thraves, Jarvis Brunby, Len Newton and Sam Wall.

Next door on the green is a pair of houses (above) one of which used to be a butchers shop. Where there is a window now was a doorway into the shop. In the centre of the building (where the down pipe is) there used to be a post box built into the wall. The property is now one dwelling.

This row of houses (left), South View, was built between 1805 and 1836 although the houses look similar they are of different ages, the pair nearest the road being the oldest.

HIGH STREET

Surprisingly for a small village there are two houses called Top House. This one at the top of the High Street (on the left overleaf) and the other opposite the school. When this house was a single dwelling, called Bradley House, Mrs Ball lived in it. She took in lodgers, mainly men who looked after the horses at the Stud Farm. When she left, Bradley House was divided to make two dwellings, the lower one retained its name and the top one became Top House. Trevor Edmundson the Head Forester moved into Top House and his assistant Bob Rowland moved in next door. It was appropriate for the Head Forester to occupy this property as at this time there was a forestry nursery at the top of the High Street and the buildings behind the houses were used by the forestry department for the nursery. Prior to that they housed horses that could not be accommodated at the Stud Farm, and earlier still, Unwin's map of 1836 shows the buildings being used as a sawmill with a sawpit and work shop. There is a beautiful building here with an overhanging stone roof. Many dwellings at the top of the High Street were in private ownership at this time. Where the trees were lined out in the nursery they have been left to grow into a plantation. When Mr Edmundson left, the Head Keeper, Tom Lord, then occupied the property until his retirement in 1963, when he moved next door. The next occupant was his successor, Dick Norris, who stayed only a short time as a bungalow was built for him at Dunsa.

The original Top House, opposite the school, is an old property that was once three dwellings. It was given the Paxton treatment at the time the village was enlarged for the second time in the 1840s. A piece of moraine debris in the form of a limestone boulder was outside this house for many years. In the 1940s the youths would return on the bus from an evening in Bakewell and occasionally in high spirits would roll the boulder down the village to the pub door. After this happened several times the council arrived to take it away. Mrs Bowering who lived at the top of High Street, in the house on the right, would not

let the boulder leave the village and had it put outside her house, where it remains. (A second boulder was on Dunsa Lane but this is now in Chatsworth garden.)

Bowering House a three storey building stood on the High Street. In this 1950s photograph it can be seen that it was shored up with timbers and of shortly after was taken down over a two year period. The Bowering family were re-housed across the road in School House now called Rock Cottage, after the moraine. The house to the right (now called Lothlorien) was re-built (below) by Bill Alexander working for Sheldon's builders and the one to the left (now called Wykewood) was re-built by Noel Yates from Great Longstone, using stone from the then recently demolished Barbrook House.

Before the Second World War only a few properties in the village had water toilets, Top House, Pilsley House (near the Farm Shop), the Devonshire Arms and the bakery. All other properties had earth closets which residents would either dig out themselves or the night soil van would collect the waste. Other household waste would be taken to a collecting area at the top of the High Street that was emptied periodically and taken to Edensor tip.

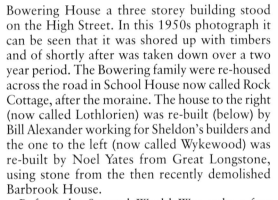

In the 1940s there were two main farms; Top Farm of 100 acres, farmed by Aubrey Broome, and The Farm (sometimes known as Lower Farm) with 75 acres, farmed by Eric Broome, bother of Aubrey. In the harsh winter of 1963, the mains water in the village froze for eight weeks but the spring that supplied the trough at the back of The Farm continued to flow. The trough was in a wall and was shared by both Top Farm (above) and The Farm (below) as their land abutted each other.

In front of Top Farm stood the snooker club. The building was not quite big enough along one wall for the cue to be lined up, so the wall was widened by the removal of mortar and a few bricks. It was subsequently taken down and the snooker table taken to the Cavendish Club in Edensor.

In 1986 the farmer vacated The Farm as the barns were falling into disrepair. These buildings, now known as Broome's Barn, behind the Devonshire Arms, were converted in 1987 to accommodate a business. The name was taken from tenant farmers that had farmed the land for two generations. Broome's Barn now comprises the showroom of Penrose Upholsters. A Chatsworth employee and his family now occupy the farmhouse and the land is farmed by the Chatsworth Farms.

Duck Row
AND AROUND THE VILLAGE

At the bottom of the High Street, beyond the Devonshire Arms is Duck Row which was once the route north east out of the village, the road now runs parallel to the Row. The string of cottages on Duck Row have dates of 1709, 1753 (and 1971) carved on massive gritstone lintels, and one is thought to have once been a smithy. These cottages are probably the oldest in the village. There are still well preserved pigsties at the end of the gardens. During the war if a pig was kept the owner had to give up their bacon ration, but they got to keep the pig! The same system operated with chickens.

In 1970/1 the backs of the cottages were taken down (left) so the buildings could be modernised whilst the fronts remained intact. When the oldest resident in the village, Mrs Tweedy, moved out of Duck Row the builders moved in.

The new backs of the cottages on Duck Row after re-building.

In this view of 1898 a thatched cottage can be clearly seen at the bottom of the High Street, on the end of Duck Row. The cottage has since been demolished.

A pile of rubble is all that remains of the cottage in this photograph dating from the 1910s. The property with the bay windows on Duck Row was once a coaching inn. The stabling at the far end of the row has now been converted into cottages.

Left: A telephone box now sits where the thatched cottage was. In front of this is the duck stone where the teenagers of the village annually erect their windmill well dressing seen here in 1991. In the early well dressings, a duck made from flowers would stand at the end of the row spouting water from its beak.

Below: On the right, next door to this cottage called Lane Side on Duck Row, was a guinea pig farm in the 1940s. Ted Ward bred up to 500 guinea pigs at a time for researchers in Sheffield to use. At night he would scythe grass from the roadside verges for fodder. Prior to this the small holders would make hay from the grass verges.

The village lanes were not overgrown and all the little narrow lanes were well used, as Pilsley was a thriving community. In the 1920s and '30s the Derbyshire County Council employed a man who had a responsibility for certain lanes in and around Pilsley. There was often a lot of loose grit on the roads as the resurfacing involved the roads being spray tarred and chippings were shovelled by hand onto the road. The road man had to keep drains and sumps cleared, and the hedges trimmed. Once a year hedge plashing (laying) was done so that the hedge would thicken from the base.

In 1950, at the 10th Dukes request, the stone from the demolished Edensor school was used to build a pair of bungalows as a memorial to his son, William Hartington, who was killed in the Second World War. The cottages, on the main road are for retired people. Each cottage has a gabled end facing forwards. On one of the gable ends in an oval 1ft 3in high with a width of 1ft there is the crest of the Coldstream Guards (below), in which both the 11th Duke and his brother served, and in the other oval is the Cavendish Crest.

Above & below: A second matching pair of cottages was built in 1970. During and after construction.

118

Well dressing today is a ritual that is largely peculiar to the county of Derbyshire, and the fringe areas, performed to give thanks for the supply of fresh water. There are several ideas as to its origin although it is thought to go back to pagan times. Some consider that the Romans introduced the custom into Britain and built altars where springs or rivers flow. Another suggestion connects the celebration with various outbreaks of plague; the wells at Eyam were used as a means of outside contact during the 1600s. The first well dressing took place in Pilsley in 1840. In 1851 a visitor to Baslow wrote of boys collecting flowers for Pilsley Tap Dressing. The early well dressings always depicted the Cavendish Coat of Arms. This image (above) is c.1880.

Right: A well dressing in 1898: l–r W. Moore, J. Bark, J. Sheldon, W. Evans, Fred Newton and Sampy Newton.

As part of the fair that accompanied the well dressings, a poster of 1906 advertises such competitions as boot cleaning for boys and knife cleaning for girls under 17 and darning a hole in a man's sock for girls under 14 years of age.

Above: Well dressing c.1900 (before the cottage was knocked down behind the dressing).

Below: Well dressing c.1912/13. Left to Right: Bill Vickers a mason at the Building Yard; Jim Bark an electrician at Chatsworth House; E. Evans, carpenter at the Building Yard; F. Haynes, gardener/handyman, groom for the Clerk of Works. ? B. Gill.

The well dressings were suspended in the mid-1910s by the 9th Duke of Devonshire after a brawl broke out between the young men of Pilsley and Baslow.

A well dressing is a mosaic picture, built up from natural materials, flower petals, seeds, grasses, leaves, tree bark, berries and moss, pressed into a base of puddled clay, which is held within a wooden frame. The tradition of well-dressing was resurrected in Pilsley in 1967. John Hughes, Head Forester, made the first frame, which had a pointed top. When he was looking for somewhere to do the petalling his assistant, Cyril Aris, offered the use of his garage and that is where the work continues to be done. The site chosen to erect the new well dressing was on the village green as it is close to the well, which is now buried beneath the Mary Devonshire Cottages. This is one of two deep wells in the village, the other being in the corner of the allotments on the High Street. Before the 20th century there was a pond on the green in front of Pool House.

By 1995 the frame was becoming unstable, and it was very unwieldy due to its size, so Ray Bradshaw designed and made a smaller one. Ray is wearing the cap and is being helped in the making of the new frame by Andy Newbould who worked in the Building Yard.

The frame is thoroughly soaked before the clay is applied. This task, which can take several days, is being undertaken in the Swiss Lake in Stand Wood, in 1991. Ray Bradshaw is looking on whilst Gordon Pearce and a visiting friend wade in the lake.

The clay has always come from a Chatsworth wood near Hassop fittingly called Clay Pits! Nowadays instead of digging a new supply each year the clay is stored and re-cycled. This saves the job of having to pick out all the small stones and pebbles. Water is added to the clay and it is puddled before being put on the frame to a depth of about one inch.

Above: Digging the clay, 1991: l-r: Laura Bradshaw, Gordon Pearce, Paul Oliver, Ray Bradshaw and Alan Back.

Below: 1995: l-r: Ann Hall, Julie, Claire & Jenny Shimwell, Ray Bradshaw, Paul White and Brian Gilbert.

Stan Miles and John Hughes drew the design for seventeen years and now Ray Bradshaw draws it; the theme is usually religious. Once it has been decided upon the picture is drawn and enlarged. It is then laid over the clay, pricked through with a needle and the outline is marked out in black wool.

Below: Kath Bosett, on the left, is assisted in petalling the frame in 1995. The design in the curve at the top depicts Edensor church with the scaffolding round it, a photograph of which is in the Edensor chapter. The text reads "I will lift up mine eyes".

Above: Liz Bradshaw on the left and Lisa Taylor are gradually filling in the picture by pressing the chosen natural materials into the clay base. All the flower petals are collected from gardens in the village, blue being the colour hardest to find. In 2004 a couple of Americans who were staying at Holly Cottage B & B had a go at petalling and this year arranged their holiday to coincide with the event so that they could help out again. On average is takes 350 hours to complete the well dressing.

Smithy House, where the work is carried out, is immediately opposite the site of the display so the job of getting the finished dressing from the garage to the site on the village green is minimised.

Right: Villagers and members of the Domain team erecting the frame on the village green in 1995.

Below: 1967 saw the revival of well-dressing in Pilsley. This was the second one in 1968. Left to right Timothy Hughes, Dale Bonsall, Andrew Link, Elizabeth Aris, Christopher Aris, Robert Hughes, Michael Hughes, Robert Hill, Chris Blackshaw, Tracy Bonsall and Dorothy Aris.

Left: The well dressing in 1970: Kath Bosett with school children: left – right standing: Deborah Mason, Maxine Drinkwater, Dorothy Aris, Joanne Oliver. Sitting: Sally Dean, Chris Hubbuck, James Hughes, Nicholas Ferguson, Paul Oliver, Stephen Knowles, Kirk Drinkwater, Stephen Aris and Mark Adams (who helped with identification of this and the previous image)

Above: Although the children previously were actively involved in the well dressing this, in 1973, was the first that they had made themselves to their own design.

Left: Children making the 1973 well dressing in the boiler house underneath the school. Since the most recent enlargement of the school the display is now made in a classroom.

Below: Left to right: Joanne Jaquest, Karen Cother, Ann Bosett, Stephen Jaquest, Linda Neave.

Above: The blessing of the wells takes place on the Thursday evening. Reverend Beddoes is seen here blessing the school well in July, 1995.

Below: The 25th anniversary of the revival of the well dressing in 1992 depicted the craft of making the display. Appropriately the image at the top is Reverend Beddoes blessing the well.

Village Fair

The blessing of the wells is the start of the three days of Pilsley Carnival, also known as Village Fair. In the early days the fair would include swing-boats and fish and chip booths which were lit by acetylene lights. The village fair started again in 1968 after the success of the school fair, held the previous year as a fund raising event on the school premises. The village fair now takes place on the village green. Dr. Wilks crowned the first carnival queen, Angie Liddicot in 1967. To the left is Margaret Wedderspoon who was one of the original carnival organisers.

Above: Watching the May Pole dancers in the school yard is Mary, Dowager Duchess of Devonshire. On the steps at her feet are members of the Aris family and in the crowd are Dorothy Gregory, Ash Withers, Jesse Grafton, Sam Burdekin and his wife, and John Hughes.

Right; In the foreground is Lady Sophie Cavendish, and her nanny (wearing the headscarf). Mary, Dowager Duchess of Devonshire is the lady wearing the wide brimmed hat.

Tug of War competitions would be between Chatsworth employees and teams from other villages. The "away" team is being watched by Pilsley lads; to the left under the tree with his arms crossed is Cliff Gilbert, Susan Bowering is leaning on the tree and standing to her right is Gordon Bowering with Mick Driscoll and Mick Bunting among the group.

The format today remains pretty much as it did in the early days except that there is no coconut shy or pot smashing stalls nowadays due to the advent of Health and Safely legislation and the closure of the Pearson Pottery in Chesterfield. There are floats, games and an array of stalls and activities. To round off the day there is karaoke in the evening.

In the 1970s Peter Swann, Matlock Town player/manager, was the "celebrity" who had the honour of crowning the Carnival Queen, Liz Aris. Peter Swann had previously played for England and Sheffield Wednesday.

The retiring Carnival Queen, Dorothy Aris, with her attendants and children in fancy dress, in July 1980. Behind her (in the tie) is Sarah Hubbuck and to her right Ann Bosett (also wearing a tie) dressed as St. Trinians' Girls. Sarah Bosett and Kerry Lubas are sporting Wimbledon attire with Stuart Fraser-Martin, to their right, dressed as Choosy Cat. Behind him is Andrew Oliver, Action Man.

Below: It rained at the 1987 Carnival.

Below: Rain is fortunately uncommon and the festivities are usually blessed with good weather.

In 1994 the 11th Duke of Devonshire crowned the Carnival Queen, Laura Bradshaw. Her attendants were to her left, Jess and Patti Doxey (to her right).

The villagers enjoy dancing and refreshments outside the pub following the blessing of the wells on the Thursday evening. Chip off the Old Cross Morris Dancers perform in 1995.

On Guy Fawkes Night the Village Fair Committee used to organise the village bonfire, together with all the necessary accoutrements: fireworks, toffee apples, bonfire toffee and soup. In 1969 it was held on the village green. One year the fire was so intense it cracked the windows in the school.

By 1994 the bonfire was held on fields down Pilsley Lane. Sadly there is no longer a village bonfire owing to safety regulations.

Left to right back row: Jenny Shimwell, Henry Sheldon, Ray Bradshaw, Alan Back, Brian Gilbert and John Norris, front row: Julie Shimwell, Mike, Greg and Ross Edwards, Keith Smith and a visiting boy.

PILSLEY CHURCH OF ENGLAND SCHOOL

Pilsley Village School was built in 1849, at a cost of £513, to a design by Paxton; there is a date stone above the entrance door. The school could accommodate 122 pupils who would have sat in rows on benches and a single fireplace provided any warmth in the main classroom. Underneath the school was another classroom. During the 1950s the school was used by the villagers for concerts, with a partition to divide the single room space and a stage was erected.

Different villagers had their own speciality acts that they would perform to entertain the audience of their friends and neighbours. Prior to the building of the Scout Hut at the top of High Street in the 1970s the school was also used by the Chatsworth Scout Troop.

The clock on the gable end is by J. Smith and Sons of Derby. The left plaque on the gable end wall reads: "1914 – 1918. This clock erected in grateful recognition of the men of this village who fought in the Great War and in affectionate remembrance of those who laid down their lives, Allan Bowering, Harry Brunby, John Fearnley, George Edward Siddall M.M."

It is interesting that until this date the Bowering family who can trace their lineage back to the 17th century spelt their name Bowring.

In 1945 there was a remembrance service for those that served and died in the Second World War and a dedication of the War Memorial. Five men are named: Gordon Bowering, William Stone, Sydney Lord, Cyril Thomas Neave and George Allen Howard. The 10th Duke of Devonshire led the dedication and the service was conducted by Reverend Hardy. Among the

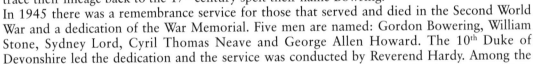

choristers were Eric and Archie Oliver. This must have been a very poignant service for the Duke and Duchess as they had lost their eldest son in the war.

The ex-service-men of the village stood together in front of the Duke. Charlie Roose's father is holding the British Legion standard.

Above: Pilsley school children c.1931/2. All ages of children attended the school, including seniors, leaving at the age of 14 to take up employment or further education.

Below: School children celebrating Coronation Day in 1953 in patriotic attire.

By 1968 the school faced closure as there were only eight pupils attending, of which four were from the Aris family. Kath Bosett was appointed temporary headteacher. The closure of Beeley school and the transfer of Pilsley's primary aged children from Baslow School helped to save it and assured Kath of a permanent post. Due to the success of the school it has been necessary to extend it more than once. An extra classroom was added in 1969 in matching materials. The windows in the main building were lowered and the large window in the southern gable end was turned into a linking door. During the building work 1 Duck Row (which was vacant) was used as a temporary school for lessons. The weathervane on top of the new classroom is in the shape of a Shetland pony.

Kath remained in charge of the school for 23 years and was succeeded by Ann Hall in 1991.

Top: The completed school in 1970.

Above: By 1974 the number of children attending the school had increased to 34 with four members of staff and a cook. Before the new classroom and the school kitchen was built the Chapel on the High Street was used as the canteen. The children would walk in a crocodile through the village at lunchtimes.

Right: The chapel is a small single storey building, built in the 1840s, that has been used as a village hall, school canteen and store. It was re-roofed in 1978 and it is now used as an annexe to the school and houses a computer suite.

The village celebrated the Queen's Silver Jubilee with a red, white and blue themed event and children's fancy dress. The Duke planted a flowering cherry tree on the school playing field. (All three villages had cherry trees; one on the pony stable ride in Edensor and one in Beeley churchyard.)

Above: Staff and children in 1991.

The Duke of Devonshire cut the ribbon and officially opened the new play area adjacent to Pilsley School in July 1995.

Behind the children are two pairs of cottages. The school head teacher traditionally lived in the cottage closest to the school and the second game keeper in the one to the far left. (The head keeper lived at Dunsa House.) A ha-ha separated the far house from the fields and lane that ran to the farm buildings beyond the village green.

In 2001 the Council for the Protection of Rural England (CPRE) awarded the most recent extension of the school a Merit Award. This award is in recognition of the excellent design which enhances the rural landscape. The awards panel was impressed by the way the extension fittingly blends with the earlier building.

Stud Farm

In 1910 the 9th Duke of Devonshire built the Stud Farm to stable his shire-horse stud. The building was made from stone that was quarried off Bradley Lane at the top of High Street. The quarry was latterly used as a tip. Annually, gypsies would visit the village and camp by Rymas Brook. Until about forty years ago they would scavenge in the tip for tin cans from which they would cut strips to make wire that secured the pegs they made.

Daily the stallions were walked through the village by the grooms in a circular route down Pilsley Lane and up the cuttings and back to the Stud Farm. The Head Groom, Mr Ball lived in Top House and Joe Newton, who succeeded him, initially lodged with the family. In the spring the stallions were walked by their horsemen to villages all around the county and beyond to serve the mares and occasionally mares were brought to the stud. The Stud Farm was still operating after the war, but the arrival of the tractor brought the demise of the shire stallion.

The 10th Duke of Devonshire was a Jersey cattle man and his herd, kept at Churchdale, near Ashford in the Water, was well known. The Stud Farm building was altered for cattle and a dairy was installed when the Duke's herd was moved to form the nucleus of the estate herd. In the mid-1950s three men were looking after the herd of 40 cows. By the 1970s this herd of cattle was becoming an expensive luxury. The present Dowager Duchess of Devonshire had become associated with the Royal Smithfield Show and decided to try selling home-grown beef and lamb for the freezer, together with dairy products from the Jersey herd. This was the start, in 1977, of the successful Chatsworth Farm Shop. It has since seen a series of expansions; the most recent in 2004 when the restaurant was created and the butchery department expanded. The Farm Shop now uses all the buildings of the Stud Farm.

THE 9TH DUKE OF DEVONSHIRE'S
SHIRE HORSE STUD
BUILT 1910
CONVERTED TO WORKSHOPS
AND OPENED BY
THE 11TH DUKE OF DEVONSHIRE
1985

On 14th June 1985 the 11th Duke of Devonshire, accompanied by the Duchess, opened the Stud Farm Workshops. Five new workshops were created in the buildings behind the Farm Shop together with a new kitchen and cold store for the Farm Shop. In 1984 Rory Penrose took up tenancy as an upholsterer (he was later to move to Broomes Barns as he outgrew the space), and the potters Simpson and Kirkland had the front unit. Three other businesses traded from the workshops.

Among the onlookers is Ted Ward, on the left, the tallest man is Roger Wardle and the three ladies at the front are from the left Mrs Dorothy Gregory (widow of Charlie – a waller), Mrs Betty Carnelley and Mrs Betty Hancock.

BIBLIOGRAPHY

Glover's Guide to Derbyshire, 1830

Kelly's Directory of Derbyshire, 1891 and 1936

Journal of the Derbyshire Archaeological and Natural History Society, Vol XLV, 1923

The Manor of Beeley	Revd. Howard Chadwick
The Architectural Review	Peter Donner, Feb 1944
The History of Chatsworth	Francis Thompson, 1949
The Buildings of England Derbyshire	Nikolaus Pevsner, 1953
A Short History of Edensor	Margaret Grayson, 1976
The Works of Sir Joseph Paxton	George F. Chadwick, 1961
The House. A Portrait of Chatsworth	The Duchess of Devonshire 1982
The Peak Advertiser, 1985	
The Estate. A View from Chatsworth	The Duchess of Devonshire, 1990
The Bachelor Duke	James Lees-Milne, 1991
The Derbyshire Village Book	Compiled by the Derbyshire Federation of Women's Institutes, 1991
Derbyshire Churchyards	Joyce Critchlow, 1993
The Fields of Beeley; A Parish Survey	Frank Robinson, 1993
Peakland Roads and Trackways	A.E. Dodd & E.M. Dodd, 1993
History of Beeley	Howard Chadwick, 1924 Edited by Chris Boyce, 1994
Joseph Pickford of Derby	Edward Saunders, 1993
Edensor 1760 – 1860. A Century of Change	Hugo Read 1995
Sheffield Artists 1840-1940	Hilary Wills,1996
Derbyshire Archaeological Journal vol. 118, 1998	Frank Robinson and John Barnatt
The Garden at Chatsworth	The Duchess of Devonshire, 1999
The Re-building of the Church of St. Peter, Edensor	Dr. Mark K. Askey, 1999
A History of Derbyshire	Gladwyn Turbutt, 1999
Chatsworth. The House	The Duchess of Devonshire, 2002
A Victorian Farmer's Diary William Hodkin's Diary 1864-66	Edited by T.A. Burdekin, 2003
A Thing in Disguise The Visionary Life of Joseph Paxton	Kate Colquhoun, 2003
Chatsworth A Landscape History	Dr. Tom Williamson & John Barnatt, 2005
Derbyshire Life and Countryside	Issues May 1989, November 1991, July 1993 and November 2003

INDEX